Generis

PUBLISHING

I0046614

Debt Recovery Process

Regulatory and Judicial Approaches

Kathleen Okafor

Title: Debt Recovery Process

Regulatory and Judicial Approaches

ISBN: 979-8-88676-140-5

Author: Kathleen Okafor

Cover image: www.pixabay.com

Publisher: Generis Publishing
Online orders: www.generis-publishing.com
Contact email: info@generis-publishing.com

Table of Contents

CAUSES OF ACTION AND LIMITATION OF ACTION FOR DEBT RECOVERY 7

Current Business Rescue Options: Alternatives to Winding-up of Companies* 13

Current Perspectives in the Recovery of Bank Loans in Nigeria 33

EFFICACIOUS AND PRAGMATIC METHODS IN DEBT RECOVERY PROCESSES 55

ENFORCEMENT OF DOMESTIC AWARDS IN NIGERIA 60

INTERLOCUTORY REMEDIES AND ARBITRATION ISSUES IN DEBT RECOVERY 68

ENFORCEMENT OF JUDGMENT AND TRANS JURISDICTIONAL ISSUES IN DEBT RECOVERY MATTERS 73

LONGITUDINAL RESEARCH INTO THE HISTORY OF DEBTS 83

PARTIES TO DEBT RECOVERY PROCESS 89

Pertinent and Pragmatic Dimensions of ADR in AMCON's Debt Recovery Process 97

Recent ADR Issues in the Recovery of Debts in Nigeria* 108

Salient Developments and Challenges in Enforcing Judgement Debts 116

SOME DEVELOPMENTS OF DEBTS PERSPECTIVES 122

The Scope and Nature of the Powers of the Board of Directors under Receivership in Nigeria. 128

CAUSES OF ACTION AND LIMITATION OF ACTION FOR DEBT RECOVERY

BACKGROUND

As economies battle variegated micro, macro economic head winds like cultural and social malaise like corruption, nepotism, gender exclusivism, political authoritarianism, so the causes of debt failure/default are different. This paper analyses the histology of debt recovery, causes of loan default and the pandemic of debt recovery. An attempt has been made to analyse the use of Asset Management Corporation (AMCON) as major debt collector in Nigeria.

1. Accrual of Cause of Action for Debt Recovery

Undoubtedly, a cause of action for debt recovery is said to accrue when the debtor defaults in payment. This was established in the case of Wema Bank Plc. v Alhaji Adisatu Owosho[1].

In the case of Kolo v. F.B.N.[2], the Court held that, it is trite law that in an action for the recovery of a debt the cause of action accrues upon demand for the payment of the debt. If no demand is made, a cause of action does not arise and no action can be commenced.[3] In the case of Ishola[4] (supra), the Supreme Court held that it is an implied term of the relationship between a banker and his customer that there should be no right of action until there has been a demand or notice given. As stated in the above authorities, it is the letter of demand from a Bank/Creditor to its customer for the payment of a debt owed in his account that gives rise to the accrual of the right of action. For the purpose of the recovery of the debt by means of the judicial process of a Court of law.[5] Until such letter of demand is issued, no right of action would arises and accrues to the bank to enable it commence a legal action in a Court of law for the recovery of the debt in question. Consequently, since the Appellant did not write and issue a letter of demand to the Respondent for the recovery of the debt allegedly owed by her. The right of action in respect of the said debt did not accrue at the time the

---

[1] (2018) LPELR-43857(CA)
[2] Kolo v. F.B.N.
[3] (2002) LPELR-7106 (CA) @ 21,(2003) 3 NWLR (Pt. 806) 216. See Ishola v. S.G. Bank (1997) 2 SCNJ, 1 @ 19, also reported in (1997) 2 NWLR (Pt. 488) 405 @ 422

[5]Angyu v. Malami (1992) 9 NWLR (Pt.264) 242 @ 252

Appellant filed the counter-claim for the debt. It may be recalled that the law is that for the purpose of the application of a limitation law, time would start to run from the date/time, a cause and right of action arises and accrues to a party.[6] Since the debt did not arise from a usual or normal banker and customer relationship service of the grant of loan, overdraft or other credit facilities by the Appellant to its customer, but arose out of alleged fraud which was discovered by the Appellant in 1999, but disputed by the Respondent, it had the duty to have formally demanded for the payment of the disputed debt from the Respondent within the time prescribed by the limitation law if it intended to use the judicial processes of a Court to recover the debt. The duty of the Appellant to comply with the provisions of the limitation law in making the demand for the payment of the debt allegedly owed by the Respondent was not left at its whims and pleasure since it is a Judicial condition precedent for the exercise of the right to claim the payment by use of the judicial process of a Court of law. The statement of account after the reconciliation by the Appellant showing the indebtedness of the Respondent to the Appellant which was disputed, did not translate or constitute a demand, as required by the law, for the repayment or payment of the debt indicated thereon. If the Respondent had acknowledged the said debt when she received it, then the acknowledgement would have activated and given rise to the right of the Appellant to claim payment by the Respondent without the need to have written a formal demand for her to do so.[7]

However, for a valid and competent legal action to be initiated and maintained by the Appellant before a Court of law, a formal demand for the payment of the debt from the Appellant to the Respondent had to be made within the period of time stipulated by the limitation law of Lagos State for actions to recover such debts between the Appellant and its customer; the Respondent. Limitation Statutes or Laws being substantive and not merely procedural and technical have to be complied with in the action by the Appellant to recover the alleged debt from the Respondent.[8] In the Hung v. E.C. Invest. Co. Nig. Ltd, it was held, that; In a claim for recovery of a debt, the cause of action accrues when a demand is made and the debtor refuses to pay.[9]

When several attempts to resolve the dispute amicably to obtain payment from a debtor failed, the creditor needs to present documentation e.g. delivery notes, invoices, written agreements, letters, emails, photographs, memos, etc.

[6] Sanda v.Kukawa L.G. (supra); Amusan v. Obideyi (2005) 6 SC (Pt. 1)147, (2005) 14 NWLR (Pt. 945) 322; Ogunko v. Shelle (2004) 6NWLR (Pt. 868) 17; Odubeko v. Fowler (1993) 7 NWLR (Pt. 308)637; Sosan v. Ademuyiwa (1986) 3 NWLR (Pt. 27) 241; W.A.P.C.Plc v. Adeyeri (2003) 12 NWLR (Pt. 835) 517.
[7] A-G Adamawa State v. A-G Federation (2014) LPELR-2322 (SC); Okonta v. Egbuna (2013)LPELR-21253 (CA).
[8] Cross River University of Tech. (CRUTECH) v. Obeten (2011) LPELR-4007 (CA).
[9] (2016) LPELR-42125 (CA). Victor v. UBA Plc. and Okonta v. Egbuna.

In the case of Josco Ag Global Resources Limited & Anor v AMCON[10] "on the duration of the substantive action in the lower Court, Counsel to the Appellant submitted that by the provisions of Paragraph 5:3 of the Practice Directions, the action in the lower Court ought to have been commenced and concluded within three months, but that the present action lasted over six months in the lower Court. Counsel stated that the lower Court ceased to have jurisdiction to adjudicate on the matter on the expiration of three months after its commencement and the judgment was therefore given without jurisdiction. Now, Paragraph 5:3 of the Practice Directions directs that a substantive action for recovery of debt should be commenced and concluded within three months. The issue of the effect of non-compliance with this provision is, however, not new and has come before the Courts.

The position taken is that the jurisdiction of the trial Court to hear and determine a debt recovery action is grounded by the Constitution of the Federal Republic of Nigeria 1999, as amended, and as well as the AMCON Act and that such jurisdiction cannot be limited, robbed, taken away by Paragraph 5:3 of the Practice Directions. Thus, non-completion of an action within three months did not take away, dent or affect the jurisdiction of the trial Court to hear and determine the matter in any way.[11]

"On the failure to commence the substantive action within fourteen days of the ex parte interim orders, Counsel to the Appellants stated that the lower Court granted the interim ex parte orders on the 17th of September, 2015 and that the Respondent, contrary to the provisions of Section 49 and 50 of the AMCON Act, failed to commence the substantive matter until the 9th of October, 2015, outside the fourteen day period stipulated in the provisions. Counsel submitted that the substantive action was thus incompetent. Section 49 of the AMCON Act reads: "1. Where the Corporation has reasonable cause to believe that a debtor or debtor company is the bona fide owner of any moveable or immovable property, it may apply to the Court by motion ex-parte for an order granting possession of the property to the Corporation. 2. The Corporation shall serve a certified true copy of the order of the Court issued pursuant to subsection (1) of this section on the debtor or debtor company. 3. The Corporation shall commence debt recovery action against the debtor or debtor company in respect of whose property an order subsists pursuant to subsection (1) of this section within 14 days from the date of the order, failing which the order shall lapse."

Section 50 of the Act reads: "1. Where the Corporation has reasonable cause to believe that a debtor or debtor company has funds in any account with any eligible financial institution, it may apply to the Court by a motion ex-parte for an order freezing the debtor or debtor company's account. 2. The Corporation shall commence debt recovery action against the debtor or debtor company

---

[10] (2018) LPELR-45637 (CA)
[11] Asset Management Corporation of Nigeria Vs Ogai Investment Co Ltd (2017) LPELR 42004(CA),
Odejide Vs Asset Management Corporation of Nigeria (2017) LPELR 42005(CA).

whose account has been frozen by a Court order issued under Subsection (1) of this section within 14 days from the date of the order, failing which the order shall lapse." The principles of interpretation of statute are so well established that they have become elementary and rudimentary. It is trite that in interpreting a statute, the duty of a Court is to consider the words used in order to discover their ordinary meaning, and then give use their ordinary meaning as they relate to the subject matter.[12] In doing so, a Court should adopt a holistic approach and interpret the provisions dealing with a subject matter together to get the true intention of the lawmakers.[13]

The Court must also not add to or take from the provisions unless there are adequate grounds to justify the inference that the legislature intended something which it omitted to express.[14] Applying these principles to the provisions of Sections 49 and 50 of the AMCON Act, it is very clear that the penalty for a failure to commence the substantive action within fourteen days of obtaining the ex parte interim orders is that the lifespan of the interim orders will lapse. It has nothing to do with the competence of the substantive action so commenced. This position is not altered by the fact that the lower Court, in making the interim order, directed the Respondent to file the substantive action within fourteen days. The directive was given in compliance with Paragraph 13:2 (3) of the Practice Directions and in furtherance of the provisions of Sections 49 and 50 of the AMCON Act. Thus, the failure of the Respondent to commence the substantive action within fourteen days of the interim ex parte did not render the substantive action incompetent. The submission of Counsel to the Appellant on the point amounted to reading words into the provisions of the Sections 49 and 50 of the AMCON Act and it was also not well founded."[15]

However, under the Failed Banks (Recovery of Debts) and Financial Malpractices in Banks Act, the Limitation laws do not apply. It states that "The provisions of the Limitation Law of a State or Limitation Act of the Federal Capital Territory, Abuja shall not apply to matters brought before the court under this Part of the Act". In the case of <u>Official Receiver and Liquidator v Moore,</u> the plaintiff bank had given overdraft facilities to the defendant. In an action brought by the bank to recover money outstanding on the overdrawn accounts the defendant maintained that, the claim was barred under the Statute of Limitation, since the last advance was made more than six years before.

---

[12] Merill Guaranty Savings & Loans Ltd Vs Worldgate Building Society Ltd (2013) 1 NWLR (Pt 1336) 581, Gbagbarigha vs Toruemi (2013) 6 NWLR (Pt 1350) 289, Commissioner for Education, Imo State Vs Amadi (2013) 13 NWLR (Pt 1370) 133.
[13] Abia State University, Uturu Vs Otosi (2011) 1 NWLR (Pt 1229) 605, Ayodele Vs State (2011) 6 NWLR (Pt 1243) 309, National Union of Road Transport Workers Vs Road Transport Employers Association of Nigeria (2012) 10 NWLR (Pt 1307) 170, Attorney General, Federation Vs Attorney General, Lagos State (2013) 16 NWLR (Pt 1380) 249.
[14] Attorney General, Federation Vs Attorney General, Lagos State (2013) 16 NWLR (Pt 1380) 249, Federal Republic of Nigeria Vs Bankole (2014) 11 NWLR (Pt 1418) 337.
[15] Per **ABIRU, JCA** *(Pp. 45-49, paras. F-D)*

"The provisions of the Limitation Law of a State or Limitation Act of the Federal Capital Territory, Abuja shall not apply to matters brought before the court under this Part of the Act". Also, section 35(5) of the AMCON (Amendment No. 2) Act, 2019; excludes the application of a Limitation law or act or similar statutes to a recovery of debt action commenced under the AMCON Act. The provision states that:

"Any statute of limitation of a state or Federal Capital Territory or any statute or rule or practice directions of any court limiting the time within which an action may be commenced does not apply or operate to bar or invalidate any claim brought by the Corporation in respect of an eligible bank asset or brought to recover a debt or enforce any security or obligation of a guarantor or surety in connection with an eligible asset".

The circumstances to the time within which an action for recovery of debt can be brought include the following:

i.   A simple contract or quasi-contract will no longer be heard by the court after the expiration of six years from the date the debt became due and actionable.
ii. Where the debt has been resolved through alternative dispute resolution and the arbitration award delivered cannot be brought before any court after the expiration of six years from the time the cause of action arose.
iii. A debt that arose as a penalty or forfeiture cannot be recovered through a court after the expiration of six years from the date the debt became due.
iv. A debt owed to a company by a member (shareholder) of the company as stated in the articles of association of the company, cannot be recovered from such shareholder after the expiration of six years from the date his debt became due.
v.   An action for account or recovery of Seaman's wages cannot be allowed in any court after the expiration of six years from the date such became due.
vi. A principal sum of money secured by a mortgage or charge on land or on any movable property (other than ship) cannot be recovered after the expiration of twelve years from the date when the right to recover such sum accrued.

Where these circumstances exist, a court will not entertain a case for debt recovery when such debt has become statute-barred. Where several attempts to resolve amicably to obtain payment, a debtor failed the creditor needs to present certain documents of dekivery notes, written agreement, e-mail, photographs, memo.

In the Supreme Court of Nigeria case between *National Social Insurance Trust Fund V Klifco Nigeria Limited*[16] **Chukwuma- Eneh JSC** contributed to this issue viz;

---

[16] **SCC 288/2015**

"What I must further state as settled law is that the Law of Limitation here has not extinguished the right to the debt; the instant debt has not been extinguished but it merely bars the right to recover the debt because of lapse of specified period of time in the law of Limitation from the accrual of cause of action. However, where there is acknowledgment of debt, which must be in writing signed by the party that is liable, the right to recover the debt by action is revived and what constitutes acknowledgment in such causes is a matter of fact in each case…"

It is elementary to state that any person who borrows money has an obligation to repay. It is only normal that the creditor should take steps to recover his money when the debtor defaults. Usually the first stage consists of writing letters requesting the debtor to satisfy his obligations, and when the debtor continues to default the creditor may take out a writ to repay the money borrowed. In **Union Bank of Nig v Penny-Mart Ltd[17],** the respondent to whom a loan was granted by the appellant bank sought a declaration that his total indebtedness to the appellant was ₦308,989.17. The Court of Appeal held that the respondent as a debtor could not sue its creditor for a declaration that he was owing the creditor a certain sum. Such a claim does not disclose a cause of action as it does not reveal what wrongful act of the creditor gave the debtor his cause of complaint.

Conclusions and Recommendation

The law has a statute of limitation for recovery of debts. A culture of borrowing is recommended and a culture of debt payment must be instilled in all for a of our human endeavor.

For developmental purposes, the law should continue to monitor borrowing, through prudential guidelines and paybacks. Appropriate sanctions should also be ensured to prevent predatory landing practices and reckless in-house/external borrowing practices.

Government and Banks need to continue publishing borrowers who fail to service their debts.

In a situation where the creditor does not recover the full debt owed within six (6) years, the creditor can still be heard by a court of competent jurisdiction as there was a break in causation.

Rule of law represents our character for civilized living. Lawyers are voices of the people. Well-trained and independent lawyers are needed more than before. Global threat of corruption undermines the independence of the judiciary over recovery of debts.

---

[17] [1992] 5NWLR (Pt 240) 228

Current Business Rescue Options: Alternatives to Winding-up of Companies*

Abstract

In Nigeria, most corporate organisations, big and small, provide for their numerous employees, families, their socio-economic environment. Consequently, when companies meet sustainability and other operational challenges, consideration of alternatives to winding up is necessary to mitigate psycho-social, unemployment and other macro-economic effects. As alternative to winding-up, business rescue have been dominant in sectors like banking, hospitality business, transport, communication and manufacturing. Essentially, the options involve companies restructuring their activities by way of take overs, mergers, reorganisations or recapitalisations due to mismanagement, predatory lending, macro-economic challenges, regulatory requirements or for strategic repositioning. Currently, local insolvency legislations like the Companies and Allied Matters Act (CAMA), Failed Banks Act (FBA) and the Investment and Securities Act (ISA), the Code of Corporate Governance provide a broad legislative framework, without much judicial certainty to guide business rescue. This paper shows the court's jurisdiction, the varieties of schemes as well as the scope and effect of business rescue schemes, worldwide. Also, this paper lists some early warning signs of the need for business rescue like inability to settle taxes, late payment of staff emoluments, defaults on interest and principal payments. The responsibilities for the internal and external restructurings processes as well as the factors to be considered in approving schemes and organising classes of interests in the company are also elucidated. There has been an attempt to create awareness amongst corporate gladiators of the alternatives to winding up and also to provide a compass for navigation of the various processes available domestically and internationally. Recent interventions of government in Nigeria have also been considered vis-a-vis the consequential impact on employees and the economy.

1. Introduction

A scheme of arrangement is a statutory procedure which is provided under the Companies and Allied Matters Act (CAMA)[18] whereby a company can make a compromise or arrangement with its members and/or creditors (or any class of them) usually to avoid insolvency or winding up. The basic question at this stage is whether the company is better alive or dead. Schemes may also be used for reconstruction of solvent companies to effect mergers, takeovers, enhance profitability, restructure debts or resuscitation of distressed companies. Accordingly, schemes are not insolvency proceedings.

There are no provisions under the CAMA that restrict the scope of a scheme. Consequently, a scheme can take various forms like compromise or arrangement about any rights on anything which the company and its creditors or members may properly agree between themselves.

Sometimes, a scheme may entail mere resuscitation of a company which is undergoing liquidation. In such a case, a company which has been dissolved may, by order of the court, within 2 years be resuscitated by take-over or merger by voiding the dissolution order on the application of the liquidator or any interested party i.e. like members or regulatory institutions[19].

Schemes have been useful to companies voluntary arrangements (CVAs) under the United Kingdom Insolvency Act 1986 because they may be informal but can bind secured and unsecured creditors as well as members[20]. Also, schemes may be used to restructure syndicated secured loans and effectuate consensual restructuring in accordance with the terms of finance documents. Usually, the signs that a company needs rescue include;

- going concern opinion by auditors,
- judgement against the company for an undisputed debt,
- refusal by creditors to restructure debts or amend credit terms following a request,
- struggling to pay creditors after issuance of pre-action letters or statutory demands,
- recurrent defaults on principal and interest payments,
- inability to settle overdue taxes, violation of loan agreements causing acceleration of debt etc.

---

*Dr. Mrs Kathleen Okafor, (Assoc. Prof.) ke_okafor@yahoo.com. **Dean, Faculty of Law, Baze University, Abuja.**

[18] Sections. 537-540, Companies and Allied Matters Act (CAMA) (Cap C20, LFN, 2004)
[19] Section 524 (CAMA)
[20] Videon A. & Turner J., Corporate Restructuring and Insolvency 2015. *The International Comparative Legal Guide to Corporate Recovery and Insolvency by Paterson S., Chapter 1, p. 1, Adebola B. "Conflated Arrangements: A Comment on the Company Voluntary Arrangements in the proposed Nigerian Insolvency Act, 2014* http://ssrn.com/abtsract_2565491

Some of the criteria or objectives for external restructuring are the following:-

- possible expansion of business,
- competition strategy
- customer retention and satisfaction,
- cost reduction
- Regulatory compliance or enhanced profitability plan.

During the schemes or even during liquidation or receivership, the directors of companies basically owe the company various duties of utmost good faith in transactions to act at all times in the company's best interest, to exercise corporate powers for the proper purpose and not for a collateral purpose[21]. Their other duties include not to fetter discretions to vote in a particular way, not to abdicate responsibility but may delegate powers, not to allow personal interest to conflict with official duties, not to make secret profit or unnecessary benefits, etc. The Nigerian Code of Corporate Governance also stipulates more elaborate duties of Directors in formulating and managing risk framework and integrity of financial reports. However, once a scheme of business rescue or full blown insolvency is initiated, the directors' duties to the company will accommodate the interest of creditors of the company and the shareholders[22]. Thus, the directors must seek to minimise losses and maximise value for the creditors[23]. The shift in directors' duties is further manifested in offences antecedent to winding-up proceedings like misfeasance, fraudulent trading, under value transactions[24], or where finances are made to creditors and not shareholders in the disposal of the company's property obtained on credit, etc. Accordingly, the court has ruled that the scheme for financial assistance for purchase of the company's own shares was not in the interest of the company[25].

2. The Basic Process of Schemes of Arrangement:-

The application for a scheme of arrangement may be made by a company, any creditor or member of the company, a liquidator or an appointed administrator. The jurisdictional powers of schemes of arrangement in Nigeria rest with the Federal High Court. The scheme requires the sanction of the court and involves two court hearings. The court performs a relatively limited supervisory role as follows:

a. An application is made to the court for an order convening meetings of the creditors and/or members (or any class of them). The application is

---

[21] Code of Corporate Governance, Act. 3 (1)(b) & (h)
[22] S. 573 (CAMA)
[23] West Mercia Safetywear v Dodd ((1988) BCLC 250, 253); HLC Environmental Projects v Carvalho (2013) EWHC 2876.
[24] Sections 502-508 CAMA
[25] Brady v Brady (1889) AC 755.

supported by a witness statement and draft explanatory statement, and the proposed scheme itself[26].

b. At the first hearing, the court will consider jurisdictional issues including whether the proposed division of the creditors and/or members into one or more voting classes appears to be proper. If satisfied that the classes are correctly constituted, the court will order that a meeting or meetings of creditors and/or members be convened to vote on the arrangement. At this stage, the court does not consider the fairness of the scheme[27]. The sanctioned meetings must be held according to the terms of the first court Order/hearing after which the scheme is voted upon by the relevant classes of creditors and/or members. A majority in number of those present and voting in person or by proxy and representing a superior majority of 75% in value of each class must vote in favour of the proposed scheme[28].

c. Sequel to the meetings, a second court hearing is held for the court to decide whether to sanction the scheme, with or without amendment. If the court decides it has jurisdiction to sanction the scheme, it would ordinarily approve the decision made at the meetings. In the case of *Re: Countrywide Financial Corporation PLC and Others*[29] where a scheme was proposed to affect a debt restructuring, the court acknowledged that: *the courts ordinarily should be slow to differ from the commercial judgement of creditors who were better placed than the courts to decide their best interests".*

Essentially, it must be noted that the second hearing is not a rubber stamping exercise and that the court will consider well established legal principles in deciding whether to sanction the scheme. The main issues to consider by the courts are usually jurisdiction, legality, minority protection and fairness. Thus, in the case of *Re: Telewest Communications Plc[30]*, the judge threw more light on the approach and stated that *"In exercising its power of sanction, the court will see first that the provisions of the statute had been complied with; Second, that the class was fairly represented by those who attended the meeting, and the statutory, majority are acting bona fide, and are not coercing the minority in order to promote interests adverse to those of the class whom they purport to represent. Thirdly, that the arrangement is such that an intelligent and honest man, a member of the class concerned, and acting in respect of his interests, might reasonably approve".* Finally, the court may order certain amendments as pre-conditions to sanction or refuse to sanction the scheme.

---

[26] In Re finance & Securities Ltd. (1993) FHCLR, 421; Andruche Inv. Plc. v Financial Mediators and 7 Ors (1993) FHCLR 51

[27] S. 539(2) & (3) ISA; Re Hawk Insurance Company Ltd (2001) 2BCLC 480.

[28] 539(2), CAMA

[29] 554, F. Supp, 2d, 1044.

[30] [2005] 1 BCLC 772; (2004) EWHE 924 (ch)

Once the sanction is granted the scheme becomes binding on all creditors and/or members regardless of notice given or not to the parties and also regardless of the fact that the creditor or member may not be known at the time[31]. In order to be valid, the court order sanctioning the scheme will be delivered to the Registrar of Companies for registration [32]. It must be understood that involvement of the Court in the process is essentially intended to ensure judicial creditors protection of members and minority interests. The company will usually remain under the management of its existing directors during the whole process and it is usually possible to combine a scheme with an insolvency process such as winding up.

Furthermore, dissenting stakeholders may, by writing to the management of the companies or liquidator, abstain from the arrangement or propose the compulsory acquisition of their securities. If the liquidator or the management takes steps that are detrimental to his/her interests, the members or creditors may make an application for necessary orders. However, the court has power to overrule dissenting stakeholders if satisfied that the proposal is fair and equitable by approving the implementation of the restructuring scheme[33].

Generally, there are various forms of schemes. The internal restructuring processes adopt principles of participatory corporate democracy of the stakeholders[34]. Some authors treat restructuring differently from business rescue. Thus, the stakeholders i.e. shareholders and creditors may resolve to survive and maintain their corporate identity and good will by;

a. Restructuring the company's ownership,
b. Changing the core business activities,
c. Adoption of new business strategy or structure, review of the economies of scale and scope,
d. Consolidation of departments,
e. bail outs,
f. debt restructuring,
g. asset stripping,
h. Labour force downsizing i.e. redundancy schemes.

Other internal restructuring schemes also involve corporate democracy of stakeholders which include the following options:

a. Reduction or increase in share capital e.g. recapitalisation,
b. Conversion of debt into shares; (partial and full),

---

[31] S. 538 & 539(3)
[32] S. 539(4)
[33] S. 538 CAMA
[34] Oladele O.O, Adeleke M.O.; The Legal Intricacies of Corporate Restructuring and Rescue in Nigeria. ICCLR (2009) 20 (5) 180-189.

c. Arrangements on sale of securities or assets
d. Scheme of Arrangements or compromise;
e. Amending class rights and preference shares to pay accrued unpaid dividends.
f. Management buy-out;

On another hand, the external Restructuring Options include:

a. Mergers[35];
b. Acquisition[36];
c. Takeovers[37];
d. Purchase and assumption of companies

3. Forms of Corporate Rescue Schemes:

State-owned enterprises, listed companies, financial institutions and other special companies which are experiencing financial difficulties may also be rescued or restructured by modern Alternative Dispute Resolution (ADR) models e.g.[38];

i. Out-of-court Restructuring: This model requires amicable, usually private out-of-court restructuring. In general, the following requirements are necessary for successful completion;

1. Proper provisions for all interested parties;
2. All important parties are actively and constructively involved in the discussion/negotiations;
3. There is an acceptable business plan for running the restructured business;
4. The company must be able to obtain funding for restructuring, in particular, there must be sufficient funds to sustain the operations of the company;

In circumstances where the debtor company can continue operations, the value of a restructured/reorganised company will usually be greater than the value of the company's assets and business if sold. Consequently, a major consideration is whether restructuring of the debtor will lead to the creation of a company of greater operational efficiency and value. However, in practice, there are some cases in which the selling off of the debtor's assets and business may be, more efficient and more economical.

---

[35] Ss. 117 & 119 (ISA)
[36] S. 538(2) Re Moorgate Mercantile Holdings Ltd. (1980) 1WLR 277
[37] S. 131. Investments and Securities Act (ISA), 2007
[38] Akingbolahun A.A. "Mediation – Based Approach to Corporate Reorganisations in Nigeria (Re: Mortgage Mercantile Holdings Ltd.). (1980), WLR, 277. 2003 – 2004. 29 NCJ Int'l Law and Comm Regulations 291, 325.

ii. Interventions by Government for Too-Big-to-Fail Companies

Government had intervened in the distress of textile industries and current estimate of government rescue intervention is about N1 trillion[39]. However, in 2018, the CBN and the National Deposit Insurance Corporation (NDIC) turned over Polaris Bank (a bridge bank) to the Asset Management Corporation of Nigeria (AMCON)[40]. AMCON had injected N786 billion into Polaris Bank, and has been searching for a credible investor in Skye Bank.

iii. Banks Rescue Schemes:-

In addition to the provisions under Part XV of CAMA on winding up of companies, banks are subject to special insolvency framework. Principally, sections 31 to 40 of the Banks and Other Financial Institutions Act, 1991 (BOFIA) and Part VIII, section 37 to 44 of the Nigeria Deposit Insurance Corporation Act, 2006, (NDIC Act), set out provisions applicable to distressed banks. The special resolution regime for banks, may be justified on a number of grounds.

1. Banks provide financial services which ensure financial system stability and drives economic growth. These services range from taking deposits, extension of credit to businesses and individuals, employment opportunities to restive youth, processing of payments, and involvement in real estate development nationwide. Failure of a systematically important bank will have more serious adverse effects on the financial system and national economy, than the collapse of a non-banking economy.

2. Bank resolution processes are more complicated than general corporate insolvency processes. In bank resolution, there is involved public interest in national development funding. Corporate insolvency processes focus on securing a collective administration of the insolvent's assets, for the benefit of the general creditors, and not economic stability.

3. Bank resolutions require timely rescue interventions, to avoid systemic ripple effect risks. Delays and compliance with general statutory procedures may exacerbate any grave situation. Sections 33 to 40 of BOFIA and Sections 37 to 44 of the NDIC Act expressly clarify the regulators responsible for initiating bank resolution processes, the grounds for initiating such processes, and the resolution measures. These provisions eliminate the risk of frivolous actions in insolvency processes, which may be detrimental to banks and the financial system.

Under Section 39 of the NDIC Act, Bridge banks were used in August 2011 for the resolution of Spring Bank (Enterprise Bank Ltd), Afribank (Mainstreet Bank

---

[39] This Day 10th June, 2018, p. 50. The Honourable Minister of Trade and Industry.
[40] Asset Management Company of Nigeria Act, 2010.

Ltd) and Bank PHB (Keystone Bank Ltd).

The advantage of bridge banks is that the special purpose vehicle results in non-disruption of banking operations. Skye Bank's depositors still had uninhibited access to their funds in Polaris Bank. This would otherwise have been difficult in a liquidation option. The debtor banks depositors would have incurred losses, as the deposit insurance maximum amount for liquidated banks is N500,000. Also, without the rescue, the employees of Skye Bank would have been laid off, and there would have been a systematic panic in the financial system, especially by illiterate traders and their informants.

As a business rescue option, the use of Bridge banks allows exemption from maintaining minimum issued/paid up capital under any extant laws. Regulators like the CAC, Securities and Exchange Commission (SEC), Nigerian Stock Exchange (NSE) etc. may provide support and grant forbearance, exemption or waivers to bridge banks in respect of their operations as provided by Section 39 (4) of the NDIC Act.

iv. Corporate Bail-outs

In comparison with Skye Bank's resolution, the recent revocation of licenses and proposed liquidation of 74 insolvent and 12 terminally distressed microfinance/primary mortgage banks and other financial institutions, by the Central Bank of Nigeria (CBN), can be adjudged fair. Obviously, these financial institutions did not pose systemic risks to the economy.

Since 2009, about N3.83 trillion of public funds have been expended on bank resolutions by the regulators in Nigeria. These business rescue schemes in banks tend to relax bank executives and increase their risk appetite based on the belief that banks are too systematically important to be allowed to fail. The Bail-outs and government rescue options have sheltered bank executives, directors and others from the adverse consequences of their breach of duties of reasonable skill and care in banks and other financial institutions. The NDIC protection was extended to 54 shareholders of Alpha Merchant Bank; Rims Merchant Bank; Commercial Merchant Bank; and Cooperative and Commerce Bank who were paid a total liquidation dividend of N2.91 million. Similarly, 631 shareholders of six Deposit Money Banks (DMBs) in-liquidation were paid a total of N2.71 billion liquidation dividend as at 31st December, 2017. As bank liquidator, NDIC also paid N6.64 billion to the Central Bank of Nigeria (CBN) as reimbursement for the unsecured amount the apex bank guaranteed to private sector depositors of five DMBs in-liquidation during the banking sector consolidation exercise[41].

The NDIC recently secured court judgement against First Bank of Nigeria

---

[41] Yebisi E.T., Omidoyi Taiye J., *Corporate Rescue Law to the Rescue of Business in Trauma in Nigeria*. Journal of Law, Policy and Globalisation, 2018, vol. 73.

(FBN) Plc. in favour of depositors of Lead Merchant Bank Limited (in-liquidation) to the tune of N556.40 million[42]. A Federal High Court upheld the priority of depositors' claims over liabilities of a bank in-liquidation.

The court held that the FBN's claim bordered on the priority of payment where a bank suspended payment or was unable to meet its obligations and that this was settled by Section 54 of BOFIA[43] which ranked depositors above claimants. Thus, the judgement of the court was aided by proper understanding of the role of NDIC status as a deposit insurer and liquidator.

v. "Bail-in" Schemes

Another current business rescue option is the Bail-in model. A bail-in involves depositors, creditors and/or shareholders of a distressed bank, fully or substantially recapitalising a distressed bank. Bail-in was used in bank resolution in Cyprus during its 2013 banking crises. In the resolution, the Bank of Cyprus converted 37.5% of deposits exceeding £100,000 into shares. A further 22.5% of the deposits were held as a buffer for potential conversion at a further date. Bail-in schemes pre-empt the use of public funds for bank resolutions, and could potentially reduce the inordinate risk appetite of bank directors. A desirable consequence of a successful Bail-in, is a healthy, revitalised bank, free from indebtedness to creditors.

Naturally, some depositors may not be willing to compromise their deposits, to save their companies or banks as alleged in the case of Skye Bank which could potentially have induced bank runs, and hastened consequential the collapse. As legally expected under section 37 of CAMA, Skye Bank's shareholders have been the residual risk bearers in the CBN's revocation of Skye Bank's banking licence and transfer of its assets and liabilities to Polaris Bank. Shareholders assume the highest risks in bad times, and receive the highest returns in good times. However, in the Skye Bank resolution, public interest required the protection of financial stability, national economy, the interest of depositors and employees to take priority over shareholders' rights which were not particularly in sync with business rescue process.

The statutory justification of the business rescue and revocation of Skye Bank's licence was premised on the legal provisions of the NDIC Act and BOFIA which empower the NDIC, in consultation with the CBN, to establish bridge banks to assume deposits and liabilities and purchase assets of failing banks. Under Section 38(1) (e) of the NDIC Act, the NDIC can "take such other measures to restructure any failing insured institution."

---

[42] 2018 CBN Annual Report
[43] Bank and Other Financial Institution Act (BOFIA) Cap B3 Laws of the Federation of Nigeria 2004

vi.   Reconciliation and Administration Processes

Companies may enter a reconciliation procedure usually where few creditors have relatively close relationships with the debtor. Reconciliation procedures are, in practice, generally controlled by the debtor and usually entail reorganisation of in-house internal and customer/supplier procedures. Also, the process is usually financed by a guaranteed bank loan or by capital provided by strategic or regulatory investors[44].

In the USA, the principal goal of Chapter 11 of the United States Bankruptcy Code is to reorganise (a scheme) the business of a company in financial distress, in order to allow it to emerge from chapter 11 as a going concern, or for the business to be sold as a going concern to realise value for its creditors. Similarly, the primary objective of administration is the rescue of the company as a going concern. However, if the administrator thinks that this objective is not feasible he may proceed to the second or third objectives of achieving a better result for the company's creditors as a whole than if the company was wound up, and (if the second objective is not feasible) the objective will be to realise the property to make a distribution to one or more secured or preferential creditors.

Procedurally, any eligible debtor may bona fide commence chapter 11 proceedings by initiating an action in court claiming that the company is insolvent on either a cash-flow or balance sheet basis. The filing of a chapter 11 petition immediately triggers off an automatic stay against any debtor who would be eligible to file an action that the company is not paying its debts. The automaticity of stay does not apply to farmers, railways and not-for-profit corporations. At least, three creditors holding in aggregate, unsecured claims of US $14,425 that are not contingent as to liability or in dispute as to liability or amount, must execute the involuntary petition. If contested, the court may not order relief unless the debtor is generally not paying its debts as they become due (such debts not being the subject of a *bona fide* dispute as to liability or amount)[45].

The scope of an automatic stay is broad and applies to almost all types of creditor actions against the debtor or the property of its estate. Particularly, the stay prevents the following events:-

- Commencement or continuation of any judicial or administrative proceeding or other action that was or could have been filed pre-petition against the debtor.
- Prevention of the enforcement of judgements to exercise control over the

---

[44] Paterson S. & Maximilian Schlote,International Comparative Guide to Corporate Recovery and Insolvency, ICLG, 2018. Chapter 1
[45] Paterson S. (ICLG) 2018, Chapter 1, p. 1.

property of the debtor or any estate, to create, perfect or enforce any lien against the property of the debtor.

vii. Restructuring by Asset or Share Acquisition; Taxes Payable:

A company may pursue business rescue by financing asset or share reorganisation or acquisition in its own company or another company. During restructuring, the company usually remains an on-going concern and the tax that applies to the restructuring procedure depends on the restructuring option chosen by the company. For the option of mergers or acquisitions, the company must first seek the direction of FIRS and obtain clearance in respect of any liabilities for outstanding corporate taxes particularly Capital Gains Tax (CGT). The tax implications during this restructuring option depend on whether the restructuring is an asset acquisition, shares acquisition or cross-border deal.

a. **For asset acquisition,** the purchaser is liable to pay stamp duties of 1.5% of the consideration on instruments executed regarding the transfer. A Value Added Tax of 5% on the consideration is also payable for such assets (if asset is not statutorily exempted). The seller is also liable to pay 10% capital gains tax realised from the sale of assets. Where the asset is land, other fees apart from stamp duties and capital gains tax are payable to the state government where the land is located. Also, the State Governors' consent fees, registration fees, stamp duties and capital gains tax on the fair market value of the property, are payable[46].

b. In a case of a **share acquisition deal**, stamp duty, value added tax and capital gains tax will not apply on the share transfer instrument. However, a nominal amount of 1000 Naira to stamp share transfer forms is payable by the company acquiring the shares. Furthermore, the share purchase agreement will also attract stamp duty which the Commissioner for Stamp Duties will assess for payment[47].

c. Where a scheme is essentially a **cross border deal** and the restructuring results in a merger with an increase in share capital then the company must up stamp[48].

4. The Responsibilities of the Process

The internal options for restructuring are each managed by the company through the general meeting of the members, the Board of Directors, and any relevant creditor or contributory Trustee/Receiver/Manager depending on the forms of scheme proposed. In the case of a compromise the creditors are the managers while arrangements are by the members or shareholders.

---

[46] Paterson S. ICLG (2018) Corporate Recovery and Insolvency. ICLG Slaughter and May Restructuring and Insolvency, (2017).
[47] Paterson S. (Ibid)
[48] Paterson S. (Ibid)

The external options involve regulatory bodies like the Securities and Exchange Commission, Creditor Banks, Corporate Affairs Commission, Asset Management Corporation of Nigeria (AMCON)[49], Nigeria Deposit Insurance Corporation (NDIC) [for Banks] [50], National Insurance Commission (NAICOM)[51] (where insurance companies are involved). Normally, internal and external restructuring exercises affirm the validity of parties' contractual and statutory obligations, as pre-existing contracts remain valid although a contract may make any event of restructuring a condition for premature termination.

Inevitably, responsibilities for both Internal and external options involve legal fees, consultancy fees, auditors due diligence costs, and in some cases, estate valuation and accounting fees, viz:

a. Mergers – are funded by all companies involved.
b. Acquisition – by all companies involved.
c. Takeovers – are usually funded by the company taking over.

5. Privity of Contract: Commercialism versus Literalism

The doctrine of privity of contract underlines business rescue arrangements which essentially enjoins investor or shareholder stewardship and finds philosophical effect on the "will theory" of contracts and economic justification in *laissez-faire* capitalism. This theory was long accepted by the courts and expressed in the second half of the nineteenth century[52]. By the theory, public policy requires that men of full age and competent understanding must have utmost freedom of contracting and that their contracts of arrangements and compromises when entered into voluntarily must be held sacred and enforced by courts of justice. Accordingly, parties, users and suppliers of capital, creditors, members are considered the best judges of their own interests, and once they voluntarily enter into any rescue contract, then the sole function of the court would be to enforce it.

However, the restrictive function of the court in the modern world to enforce voluntary contracts has been made subject to public policy, national security, economic exigency which challenges the traditional theory of unrestricted freedom to contract. In relation to business rescue schemes, the freedom of choice has been whittled down from many dimensions by government regulations, nationalistic, anti-trust, and paternalistic ideals[53].

---

[49] Asset Management Corporation Amendment Act of Nigeria Act 2015 (AMCON Act).

[50] Nigerian Deposit Insurance Act (No. 16) 2006 (NDIC Act),

[51] National Insurance Commission Act, 1997 (NAICOM Act).

[52] Atiyah P.S., The Rise and Fall of Freedom of Contract, 1979, Oxford University Press.

[53] S. 121 ISA Act, Public Enterprises (Privatisation and Commercialisation Act, (1999) Cap 346 LFN (1990).

In terms of contractual interpretations, there has been the perception that courts are moving away from literalism and placing increased emphasis on commercial contexts of schemes as voluntarily espoused by businessmen. In *Re: Sigma Finance Corp[54]*, the receivers sought the guidance of the Supreme Court on how to pay off the secured creditors. Four out of five Supreme Court Justices reversed the Court of Appeal's decision and accepted a "business common sense" approach to contractual interpretation, rather than a "detailed semantic analysis". In summing up the essence of the judgement, Lord Collins stated that "the instrument must be interpreted as a whole in the light of the commercial intention which may be inferred from the face of the instrument and from the nature of the debtor's business"[55].

The Supreme Court judgement in *Rainy Sky SA v Kookmin Bank[56]* recently confirmed the courts' attitude and approach. The Supreme Court held that the ultimate aim of interpreting a provision (especially) in a commercial contract is to determine what the parties mean by the language used. This involves ascertaining what a reasonable person would have understood the parties to have meant. The relevant reasonable person in the case being someone with all the background knowledge reasonably available to the parties at the time of the contract[57].

The above recent case of *Rainy Sky* patently supported and expanded on the conclusions drawn by the Court of Appeal in *HNY Luxembourg Sarl v Barclays Bank Plc.* [58] In this latter case, the court considered two conflicting interpretations of a clause in an inter-creditor agreement. The clause concerned the ability of a secured trustee to transfer the liabilities of the lenders and to release the security and guarantees given by various members of the group. The respondents contended that the wording of the clause permitted the security trustee to release from security or liabilities only the very entity whose shares were being sold i.e. the Obligor or Obligor's holding company. The Appellants argued that the wording permitted release of an Obligor where the shares of the Obligor itself or the shares of the Obligor's holding company were being sold[59].

The court looked beyond the plain "natural meaning of the words" and formulated the idea that had the parties wanted to include the concept of a sale of subsidiaries' assets then it would have been easy enough for them to do so expressly. The court particularly made the point that "when alternative constructions are available one has to consider which is the more commercially sensible"[60].

---

[54][2009] UKSC 2
[55] In Re: Sigma Finance Corp. Supra. (2009) UKSC 2.
[56][2011] 1 UKSC 50
[57] Rainy Sk v Kookmin Bank, Supra.
[58] [2010]EWCA Civ 1248.
[59] Slaughter and May, 'Insolvency law and Contract: Policy and Practice in the US and UK'.
Comparative Legal Guide to Coprorate Recovery and Insolvency (2012). GLG, London.
[60] HNY Luxembourg Sarl v Barclays Bank Plc.

In summary, the trend shows that where there are conflicting interpretations of any clause in business rescue options, the court will lean towards the less literal interpretation if it accords with the purpose of the agreement, the knowledge of the parties and commercial sensibilities. Thus, the principle of freedom of contract may be relegated in business restructuring for commercial realism and national efficacy as in the business rescue of Skye Bank.

6. Organisation of Voting Classes and the Classic Test of Interested Creditors

In restructuring, there may be many voting classes. Thus, the process of constituting voting classes involves presenting an application to the court for direction as to the procedure or manner of the meeting or meetings of the scheme to be presented to the creditors or shareholders for approval. The court, when deciding whether to grant leave to convene the meeting of creditors (or members), will consider the constitution of the class or classes of creditors. The court will also consider whether or not the necessary majority is likely to be obtained at any meeting. In *Premacon Holdings GmbH v Credit Agricole*[61] *(Primacom),* the court considered that it did not have before it evidence to categorically conclude that there was no hope of the scheme progressing, and so gave leave for the meetings to be convened.

The practice by English courts is to usually ensure that any issues as to classes are raised at the first hearing[62]. This approach potentially allows issues to be identified and resolved early in the proceedings. The responsibility for determining the identity and the classes of the creditor lies with the applicant. The applicant is expected to bring to the attention of the court at the earliest possible opportunity, any issues that may arise relating to the constitution of the classes. If applicants are able to show that certain classes of creditors will not be affected by the scheme (usually on the balance of probabilities), they (applicants) may be able to ignore some creditors particularly those opposing the arrangement or compromise.

Pertinently, only creditors who may be affected by the proposed scheme should be consulted. In *Re Bluebrook Ltd and others*[63] a scheme to effect a debt restructuring was presented. The court confirmed that a creditor will not be affected if it had no real economic interest in the corporation. In that case, a current "going concern" valuation (rather than a liquidation valuation or a future valuation) was held to be an appropriate test to demonstrate economic interest such that certain creditors were held to have no interest in the scheme.

---

[61] [2011] EWHC 3746 (Ch)
[62] Paterson S. Ibid
[63][2009] EWHC 2114

The various classes of creditors in the corporation are mainly secured, unsecured and preferential. The court usually applies a broad view of interested creditors but the classic test is as stated in *Sovereign Life Assurance Co v Dodd*[64], namely that the class must be confined to those persons whose rights are not so dissimilar as to make it impossible for them to consult together with a view to their common interest. This was considered in detail in *Re: Hawk Insurance Company Limited*[65]. The English court of Appeal stated that the question to consider was whether the rights of those who are affected by the scheme proposed are such that the scheme can be seen as a single arrangement or that the scheme ought to be regarded, on a true analysis as a member-linked arrangement. The court agreed that the answer to the above question involved an analysis (i) of the rights which are to be released or varied under the scheme, and (ii) of the new rights (if any) which the scheme gives, by way of compromise or arrangement, to those whose rights are to be released or varied. As in *Primacom,* the crucial factor is to consider creditor's common rights rather than their interests.

7. The Factors for Approving Schemes

After satisfying itself of its jurisdictional powers to sanction a scheme and compliance of CAMA and other regulations (provisions), the court will also consider other factors like constitution of classes, proper and adequate notice of the meetings and appropriate or sufficient information to enable those voting to make an informed decision, and whether the resolutions to approve the scheme were properly passed. If all compliances are met then, the court would exercise its discretion considering the following factors:

- Whether approving the scheme is fair and reasonable in the circumstances. The court must be satisfied that the proposed scheme is such that, objectively *"any intelligent and honest man, a member of the class concerned, acting in respect of his interests might reasonably affirm"*. Once the scheme appears fair and reasonable, the court will not delve into commercial considerations of the scheme.
- Whether each class is reasonably represented by those attending the meeting and that the statutory majority acted in good faith. This requires consideration of whether sufficient numbers of creditors in each class meeting voted at that meeting in person or by proxy so that the court can be satisfied that the outcome represents a true decision of the relevant class.
- Whether there are pending issues of Recognition orders of securities or other assets, like real estate situated in the local jurisdiction.

---

[64][1892] 2QB 573
[65][2001] 2 BCLC 480

27

- Whether the controllers of the company are amenable to orders or directions of the court e.g. where the administrator is responsible for running the company, and practically controls the company or where the debtor is responsible for running the company, and controls the management, higher level organisations and institutional investors, holding companies, or supervisory agencies may also in practice control the company.
- Whether there are other orders necessary during the restructuring e.g. new investors in the debtor company may defer payment of dividends during restructuring, or the restriction of share transfers in the debtor company to third parties, unless permitted by the court.

8. The Legal Effects of Business Rescue on Corporate employees?

When a company undergoes restructuring, the employees may be terminated or transferred to a resultant organisation. In Nigeria, there are no laws which mandate companies to retain all existing employees following restructuring. However, the Labour Act states that trade unions and worker's representatives (in strategic sectors without unions) must be informed of redundancy and severance packages[66]. The allowances, benefits and terminal benefits and pension allowances of disengaging staff must be paid before the disengagement of the staff affected.

Prior to the approval of a restructuring scheme, the law requires that SEC will consider the effect of the restructuring exercise on the company's employees. At the end of the restructuring exercise, the company must submit to SEC evidence of settlement of severance benefits of disengaging employees. Furthermore, the NSE Rulebook requires listed companies who intend to restructure to include a statement on the impact of the intended acquisition on its employees and the continuity of the business. The information is to be disseminated by circulars submitted to the NSE and distributed to shareholders.

In Nigeria, the initiation of insolvency proceedings automatically translates to the services of the employees being no longer required and thus terminated. Thus, downright liquidations tend to exacerbate the unemployment crises and social malaise already in Nigeria. Under CAMA, employees wages or salaries, pension allowances, accrued holiday remunerations and employee compensation rights are given preferential treatment and are paid in priority to all other creditors[67]. Employees who are terminated due to insolvency cannot bring an action for wrongful termination but can institute an action regarding unpaid entitlements.

---

[66]S. 20, Labour Act, Cap 198 (LFN) 1990
[67] S. 494 CAMA

The priority ranking provided under CAMA is contentious in view of the BOFIA[68] and Failed Banks Act which give priority to liquidation costs[69]. Consequently, one can reason that the priority of employees' emoluments operate outside the legal framework of banks recovery.

9. Contractual Rights and Party Autonomy

One question which inevitably arises is whether the initiation of business rescue can stay proceedings or contractual rights. In the case of *Re Olympia & York Canary Wharf Limited*[70], the court considered the issue of the moratorium on "other proceedings... execution... or other legal process" under section 11(3)(d) of the Insolvency Act, 1986. In particular, the court considered whether the phrase did not extend to "the taking of non-judicial steps such as the service of a contractual notice" as to allow parties to terminate contracts with the debtor during its administration. The court decided that business rescue stay proceedings or other legal process serve as stay on contracts termination provisions, as demonstrated in the case of Lehman Brothers Holding Inc.[71]

In *Belmont Park Investments Pty Ltd v BNY Corporate Trustee Services*[72], there was no direct *ipso facto* equivalent in the UK. However, the courts considered the priority of payments and the subordination provisions in the light of the anti-deprivation principle. The anti-deprivation rule states that "no person possessed of property can reserve that property to himself until he shall become bankrupt and thereafter it shall pass to another and not his creditors". Thus, the court extensively analysed the anti-deprivation principle which applies to all reconstructions and arrangements and the historical body of case law (dating back to the eighteenth century) supporting it. It was concluded that for the anti-deprivation rule to apply, there must have been a deliberate intention of the party to evade insolvency law and the application of commercial sense was a "highly relevant factor" for considering encroachment into the arena of freedom of contract. The Judge acknowledged that: "Despite statutory in roads, party autonomy is at the heart of English commercial law... And there is a particularly strong case for autonomy in cases of complex financial instruments such as those involved in this appeal". The court stressed that "this was a complex commercial transaction entered into in good faith". The subordination provisions were held to be valid and enforceable.

The conflicting outcomes of *BNY* and *Belmont* are surprising because both cases stem from two jurisdictions with insolvency regimes which have the same

---

[68] S. 54 BOFIA
[69] S. 20 & 21 of the Failed Banks Act
[70] [1993] BCC 154
[71] Lomas and Others (as Joint Administrators of LEHMAN Brothers International) V JFB Firth Rixson Inc. (2012) EWCA, Civ 419 (3rd April, 2012).
[72] [2011] UKSC 38

objective of rescuing companies in financial difficulties. Both the *ipso facto* rule and the anti-deprivation principle have the same goal of protecting the value of estates. Undoubtedly, the *ipso facto* rule in the United States results in the interference with contractual rights whilst the anti-deprivation rule in England, construed narrowly is subject to good faith and commercial sense. One can safely conclude therefore that English law recognises the continuing importance of freedom of contract as the foundation of the English commercial law which is the position of inherited English Law in Nigeria[73].

Furthermore, in the United States insolvency regime, the case of *Lehman v JFB Firth Rixson Inc.*[74] is relevant. The case concerned interest rate swaps governed by the International Swaps and Derivative Association (ISDA) 1992 Master Agreement. Each party's obligation to make payments to the other party was subject to the condition precedent that the other party was not in default (insolvency constituting an event of default) by virtue of section 2(a)(iii) of the Agreement. The American Court of Appeal found that the anti-deprivation principle was not contested and that the indefinite suspension of the payment obligation of the non-defaulting party might be criticised as imperfect but, following *Belmont,* it could not be said to be uncommercial. Lord Justice Longmore stated that he could see no reason why the law should preclude two commercial parties from negotiating such a clause. He found that "It is a prudent limitation on the duration and operation of the contract".

A balance must be achieved by US, UK and Nigerian laws between[75] creditor protection and achieving the primary purpose of facilitating the rescue of companies. Thus, a key requirement for a successful restructuring remains contractual stability, party autonomy and adoption of the principle of commercialism.

Recommendations and Conclusions

1. Current insolvency framework is wrongly predicated on the assumption that the company is failing and the business is beyond recovery. This is in contrast with the modern insolvency law trend which leans towards business rescue and restructuring.
2. Schemes of arrangements under the CAMA and other statutes provide flexible models for rescuing companies. Schemes are particularly attractive and most commonly encountered where directors can remain in control of the company and avoid the need for insolvency.

---

[73] Mba, S. U., Rethinking Business Rescue in Nigeria: Borrowing Virtues from Chapter 11 of the Bankruptcy Code Collection of Central European University of Legal Studies, Budapest, Hungary 2015.
[74] [2012] EWCA Civ 419
[75] Metavante Corporation v Emigrant Savings Bank No. 09 – 3007, (7th Cir 2010)

3. There is a current trend in insolvency laws for the courts and the legislature to respect the fundamental principle of freedom of contract which are manifest in business rescue options. Understandably, there is general reluctance by the law to allow unlimited parties' rights to contract freely for nationalistic purposes.

4. Under Nigerian law, creditors' right cannot basically be compromised by a contract to which they are not a party to. Consequently, offshore schemes involving multinational companies which propose to alter the rights of local secured creditors without their consent could be considered contrary to public policy.

5. Nigerian laws on priority of interest need to be harmonised with international provisions to enhance foreign investments.

6. Pre-insolvency breaches under sections 501 – 507 CAMA are wide and include simple refinancing which could be termed inducing credit to the company by false pretence or fraud, or causing transfer of a charge on the company's property[76], or misapplication of company's money or property which can hamper genuine business rescue attempts. The law should therefore, provide specific guidelines for business rescue schemes to avoid the misconception of business rescue schemes as fraudulent trading.

7. There are many conflicting judicial positions and administrative scenarios for business rescue. The Supreme Court of Nigeria should lead in the reconciliation of the legal grounds of business rescue and the limits of party autonomy for certainty.

8. As Nigeria seeks efficient international inclusionism, there is need to harmonise Nigerian rules on priority of debt securities under CAMA, NDIC Act, BOFIA with the Unidroit and UNICITRAL Rules.

9. The Courts and government agencies should be more creative in quick business rescue interventions to enable directors and shareholders take quick commercial decisions to save jobs and social disruptions.

10. Of greater concern is that Government must maintain micro and macro-economic indices, political stability, infrastructure enhancement as well as eradicate corruption to enhance business profitability to pre-empt most unnecessary and expensive business rescue activities.

11. To minimise failures, more frequent regulatory monitoring and timely remedial business schemes must be initiated by the shareholders, creditors the CAC, SEC and the CBN (for Banks).

12. Judicial efficiency is required for expeditious conclusion of managerial breaches as a deterrent to future collapses. Criminal civil and restitutive processes should all be pursued vigorously to sustain development goals.

13. Corporations create wealth for all nations and pioneer development and research. Their rescue should be of greater governmental concern and Nigeria's poverty levels will be regressed.

14. Professional bodies like the Nigerian Bar Association (NBA), Institute of

---

[76]s. 506. CAMA

Chartered Accountants of Nigeria (ICAN), Institute of Directors (IoD) and Chambers of Commerce should jointly formulate various forms and processes to aid the court in quicker dispensation of business rescue options.

Current Perspectives in the Recovery of Bank Loans in Nigeria*

Abstract

Prior to the independence of Nigeria in 1960, commercial lending in Nigeria was basically non-existent as the economy was mostly subsistent agriculture. However, the growth of trade between the United Kingdom and the West African sub-region inevitably led to the establishment of the African Banking Corporation in 1891 by Elder Dempster Company, a shipping conglomerate in Lagos, Nigeria. Progressively, many corporations in manufacturing, telecommunications, banking, oil and gas, retail and other businesses merged and started utilising facilities of banks for expansionary purposes or for other operational purposes. However, due to frequent policy somersaults, poor management, predatory lending practices, general economic meltdown and macro-economic headwinds, companies started defaulting on the facilities and the creditors have had to realise their securities. Some of the statutory provisions and cases on the process and laws on recovery of debts have been subjected to conflicting interpretations partly because of the multitude of institutions and laws on the subject. Nevertheless, there is the underlining objective of maintaining the principle of separate legal entity of companies and also ensuring that creditors assets are recovered. This paper essentially considers the laws and cases and the emerging framework of realisation of secured and unsecured credits. In this paper, there is focus on bank lending and the institutional regulations which have developed as a result of growing Non-Performing Loans (NPLs) and bank failures.

1. Introduction

The Structural Adjustment Programme in Nigeria in 1986 resulted in increased investor participation in the banking industry which increased the number of banks over a 10 year period. By 1995, the number of distressed banks had increased to 60, out of which 31 were terminally insolvent[77]. This scenario

*Dr. Mrs Kathleen Okafor, (Assoc. Prof.) Dean of Law, Baze University, Abuja.
ke_okafor@yahoo.com.
[77] CBN Annual Report 1995

generated many non-performing loans (NPLs) which represented as much as 44 per cent of total loans disbursed. Distressed banks accounted for 60.82% of the total NPLs in the Nigerian banking industry which clearly indicated a link between NPLs and bank failures[78].

The various factors which contributed to the banking crisis included unprofessional lending practices, mismanagement of the banks, and general operational corruption in national activities, management's inordinate appetite for profit maximisation, capital inadequacy and also general inefficient economic management. To salvage the situation, the Nigerian Deposit Insurance Corporation was set up in 1988 mainly as a guarantor of bank deposits and also to prevent the demise of banking institutions. The Failed Banks (Recovery of Debts) and Financial Malpractices in Banks Decree was promulgated in November 1994 with Failed Banks Tribunal set up to recover debts owed to banks and to punish the perpetrators of inefficient lending practices in banks through the introduction of special proceedings to expedite trial of cases falling under the Decree.

By 1999, over 45 criminal cases and 672 debt recovery cases were concluded under the provisions of the Decree before the replacement of the Decree with the Failed Banks (Recovery of Debts) and Financial Malpractices in Banks Act[79].

Nevertheless, bank loans to the economy as at the end of 2015 hovered around N13.1 trillion with the ratio of non-performing loans to total credit arising to 11.7 per cent as at the end of June 2017 from 5.3 per cent. The balance sheets of most deposit money banks (DMBs) became seriously jeopardized[80] due to humongous debt overhang of NPLs partly due to depreciation of the naira and depression leading debtors to default on servicing foreign currency-denominated loans. These lending practices put depositor's funds at risk thereby disrupting the lending cycle needed for economic development.

2. Statutory Framework

Presently, there are many enactments which regulate recovery of bank loans in Nigeria. These include the Companies and Allied Matters Act (CAMA), The CBN Act, the Investment and Securities Act (ISA Act) with the Securities and Exchange Commission Rules 2013, the Banks and Other Financial Institutions Act BOFIA in relation to licensed banks and other financial institutions, the Nigerian Deposit Insurance Corporation (NDIC) Act, the Assets Management Corporation of Nigeria (AMCON) Act which resolves banks' non-performing loans/assets, the Failed Banks (Recovery of Debts and Financial Malpractices in

---

[78] CBN Annual Report 2010
[79] FBA Act
[80] NDIC Annual Report 2017

Banks Acts (FBA) 2004, and the recent Secure Movable Assets Acts 2017).

Firstly, the **Companies and Allied Matters Act (CAMA)**[81] broadly outlines the procedures for all corporate insolvency to protect the assets of companies in liquidation and also ensure proper and orderly disposition of debts/liabilities[82]. In the case of banks, the dominant objective of the laws is to protect depositor's interests and retain public confidence in the financial system.

Section 414 of CAMA broadly provides the process of winding up of all insolvent companies which also applies to failed banks to protect the depositors and creditors of Failed Banks in liquidation. Section 414 of CAMA provides that "where a company is being wound up by the court, any attachment, sequestration, distress or execution put in force against the estate or effects of the company after the commencement of the winding up shall be void".

Section 417 of CAMA provides that, "If a winding up order is made or a provisional liquidator is appointed, no action or proceedings shall be proceeded with or commenced against the company except by leave the court on such terms as the court may impose". Accordingly, s. 417 safeguards the interest of creditors as a whole as a matter of public policy which means that action may be commenced against a failed bank once the NDIC has been appointed as provisional liquidator. The creditor can only bring a claim before the liquidator with leave of court to execute any judgement and existing proceedings against the failed bank must be stopped.

Under section 500 (1) OF CAMA[83], "where a creditor levies execution against any goods or land of a company or attaches any debt due to the company, and the company is subsequently wound up, the creditor shall not be entitled to retain the benefit of the execution or attachment against the liquidator in the winding up of the company unless he has completed the execution or attachment before the commencement of the winding up.

Section 500 (1) (c) CAMA however states that; "… the rights conferred by this subsection on the liquidator may be set aside by the court in favour of the creditor to such extent and subject to such terms as the court thinks fit".

Section 500 (2) CAMA defines what amounts to completion of an execution or attachment as follow: *"For the purposes of this section, an execution against goods shall be taken to be completed by seizure and sale, and on attachment of a debts shall be deemed to be completed by receipt of the debt, and an execution against land shall be deemed to be completed by seizure and, in the case of an equitable interest, by the appointment of a receiver".*

The summary of these provisions is that the court can in its discretion set aside any liquidation and permit the creditor to retain the benefit of the execution or

---

[81]**Companies and Allied Matters Act** CAP. C20. L.F.N. 2004 (CAMA)
[82] S. 401 – 531 CAMA
[83] **Section 24 of the Asset Management Corporation of Nigeria Act, 2010 (AMCON Act).**

attachment of its judgement against the failed bank. Thus, in the case of *Federal Mortgage Bank of Nigeria v NDIC (Liquidator of United Commercial Bank Limited) in Liquidation,* the Federal Mortgage Bank of Nigeria (FMBN) as the creditor, obtained judgement against the United Commercial Bank Limited (UCML). FMBN levied execution and attached UCBL's movable assets on the 5th of September 1994, and the Deputy Sheriff attached the assets with UCBL's premises. Four days later, UCBL's banking licence was revoked, and the NDIC was appointed a liquidator and assumed control over the assets of the bank including the attached assets. FMBN subsequently applied to the High Court for an order compelling the liquidator to produce the attached assets of the bank and to direct the deputy sheriff to sell same. The Supreme Court decided that where execution and attachment of a bank's asset have been carried out, but the appointment of the liquidator occurs prior to the sale of the assets, any such execution or attachment would be deemed to be inchoate, and thus falls within the ambit of **Section 414 of CAMA,** which renders the action void.

Furthermore, under **section 501 (1)** of CAMA where the assets of the company have been taken by a deputy sheriff in execution of a judgement or an order of court, and prior to the completion of execution a notice is subsequently served on the sheriff that a provisional liquidator has been appointed, the sheriff is mandated to deliver the assets to the liquidator.

These general insolvency laws seek to protect the interest of creditors as a whole, by preventing a single creditor who through an execution of a judgement obtained from a court of competent jurisdiction from receiving full payment of his claim at the cost of the claims of other creditors. The common law case of **Walker v Syfret**[84] supports the statutory provision of CAMA in that, a sequestration order which includes an attachment order or judgement crystallises the insolvent's position; the hand of the law is laid upon the estate and at once, the rights of the general body of creditors have to be taken into consideration. Thereafter, no transaction can be entered into with regard to the estate matters by a single creditor to the prejudice of the general body. Applying these provisions to failed banks, in contrast with regular companies, the creditor's primary focus and the NDIC as liquidator for banks, is to mainly secure and satisfy the deposit liabilities of the failed bank in liquidation.

The importance of this section is that once a winding up order is made, or where a provisional liquidator has been appointed to liquidate the assets of the company, no action against the failed bank can be commenced, neither can any on-going proceedings be continued except with the leave of the Federal High Court[85] subject to such terms as the court may impose[86]. The Banks and Other Financial Institutions Act[87] (BOFIA) also provides that, no suit shall be

---

[84] (1911) AD 141, Par. 166
[85] **Section 417 CAMA**
[86] *NDIC VS Alhaji Mohammed & Ors (2018) LPERL-44744 9 CA.*
[87] S. 41 BOFIA

instituted against a bank whose control has been assumed by the NDIC and if any such proceedings are instituted in any court or tribunal against the failed bank, it shall abate, cease or be discontinued without further assurance other than by this Act[88].

a. The Failed Banks Act

Section 2 of the Failed Banks Tribunal (Consequential Repeal, etc.) Act No. 62 of 1999 abolished the Failed Banks tribunals. The Failed Banks Decree was later repealed by the Failed Banks (Recovery of Debts) and Financial Malpractices in Banks Act (FBA).

i. Jurisdictional Issues:

Section 1 of the Act vests the Federal High Court with exclusive jurisdiction in any action for the recovery of any debt owed to a failed bank and the jurisdiction conferred by the Act cannot be ousted by the agreement of the parties or by the provision of any other law. Under section. 1 of the Failed Bank Acts, the jurisdiction of the courts is as follows:

> The Federal High Court in this Act referred to as "the Court" shall have power to
> *"recover, in accordance with the provisions of this Act, the debts owed to a failed bank, in the ordinary course of business and which remain outstanding as at the date the bank is closed or declared a failed bank by the Central Bank of Nigeria;"*

Thus, the Federal High Court is empowered "to recover, in accordance with the provisions of this Act, the debts owed to a failed bank, arising in the ordinary course of business and which remains outstanding as at the date the bank is closed or declared a failed bank by the Central Bank of Nigeria."

Section 1 (3)(a)(c) and Rule 17 of the Failed Banks Act provide for proceedings to be conducted in a manner to avoid undue delay. Accordingly, hearing may continue on a day to day basis. It is noteworthy that this provision has not reduced cases and adjournments.

ii. The main Objectives of the Failed Banks Act include:
- To assist in resolving distress of failing banks through speedy recovery of their non-performing loans arising in the course of business and which remains outstanding as at the date the bank is closed or declared a failed

---

[88] S. 41, **Banks and Other Financial Institutions Act.** CAP B3. LFN, 2004.

bank.

- To sanitize the banking sector through criminal prosecution and conviction of errant directors found guilty of banking malpractices.
- Speedy trial of offences relating to financial malpractices in banks and other financial institutions as specified in the Act or such other offences relating to the business or operation of a bank under any enactment.

iii.   Provision for Lifting the Corporate Veil

Under Section 1 (3) (b) (ii) of the Act, the court may lift the veil of a company which is owing a failed bank to trace the representatives and assets of the failed financial institution. The veil of incorporation will be lifted to hold the directors, shareholders, and corporate officers of failed banks connected with the granting of the loan, liable for an unsecured debt, or the security is impossible to locate, or the identity of the debtor is difficult to locate, or the debtor is non-existent, fake or fictitious or in any way unidentifiable. Under Section 12(2) thereof, the court can proceed to recover from such officers of the failed bank jointly and severally, the outstanding loan and interest.

iv.   Proof of the Debt

The Failed Bank Act grants power to the Court to control the property of a debtor where the court is satisfied that a prima-facie case has been made out against a person to prohibit disposition of property movable or immovable, stop outward payments, operations or transactions (including any bill of exchange) for the time specified and grant interim measure of protection pending the determination of the proceedings. Nigerian rules on insolvency do not seem to contemplate specific provisions on the certainty of the date of document. Indeed, there is no need to prove date certain as applies in Italian law. The Nigerian rules appear to be less stringent in that proof that a payment or transaction occurred before insolvency may be given with any means, including by alleging factual elements and circumstances which may demonstrate anteriorly to insolvency regardless of date certification by public authorities. This position is somewhat similar to the open clause encompassed in the second part of section 2704 of the Italian Civil Code allowing case law to establish other equivalent instances' where the date can legally be considered certain.

In the United Kingdom, and Italy, filing proof of claim in administration or liquidation proceedings, entails filling in a form and filing documents in support of the claim. The liquidator may request for further proof and documents thereof. A creditor has a right to challenge the denial or admission of the claim. However, there appears to be no basic need to prove date certain anteriority to insolvency in Nigeria. Under English law, it is not necessary that a contract should be dated to be valid. Nor is it necessary for an officer of the insolvent company to be physically present once there is acceptance, consideration and the intention to create legal relations between the parties, and delivery of the deed. If an issue arises on the date of the document, reference can be made to other elements connected to the formation thereof in order to establish timing.

Similar conclusions may be drawn on the U.S. approach to the problem. No date certain requirement is contemplated in Title 1 of the U.S. Bankruptcy Code, neither in Chapter 7 (liquidation), nor in Chapters 11 and 13 (reorganisation). As far as pre-petition claim for proof of debt in bankruptcy is concerned, there is a presumption of validity of the claim and supporting evidence thereof, and in principle debtors will hardly question the date or validity of the documents filed with the claim.

The French legal system, which for a number of historical reasons appears to bear the most similarities to the Italian and Nigerian ones does not seem to contemplate a date certain concept. The existence, date and validity of claims/debts under French insolvency law are matters of proof. There are no specific rules concerning the date certain within the framework of insolvency proceedings. Creditors must file a declaration of claims/debts (*declaration de creance*) with the creditors' representatives within a specific time period (2 months for French creditors). The claims/debts are verified and paid in accordance with the rules applicable to the insolvency proceeding. The notarisation or the registration of an agreement attributes certainty as to the date of the covenant giving *"date certaine"* to the document and overturning the burden of proof for challenging the date of the claim/debt. Even if this element may strengthen the claimant's position, it is not essential, in that claims/debts which do not have "date certain" can also be accepted if they are clearly evidenced.

Under section 1 (4) of the Failed Banks Act, the court may admit and act on any evidence which it considers relevant in any civil and criminal proceedings notwithstanding that the evidence was inadmissible under any other law or enactment. This provision is controversial but the court is given the power to consider the weight of evidence to be accorded to such evidence. Also, primary and secondary evidence may be used to establish the loan and that the payment is due.

To aid the courts in dispensation of debt recovery, Section 6 of the Failed Banks Act provides as follows:

(a) The examination reports and recommendations of the Central Bank of Nigeria or the Nigeria Deposit Insurance Corporation or their joint examination reports and recommendations; or

(b) Any report of the Central Bank of Nigeria or the Nigeria Deposit Insurance Corporation

(c) The report of a person appointed by the Central Bank of Nigeria or the Nigeria Deposit Insurance Corporation, on the financial condition of a Failed Bank shall be sufficient proof that a loan or advance is owed to a failed bank and is due for recovery under those Acts.

This provision is salutary as assembling primary evidence of the debt had been onerous because of operational negligence, deliberate destruction of evidence, and administrative lapses by financial institutions. Usually, errant officers had left the bank and the Courts continued to require statements of account as required under the Evidence Act to prove indebtedness and explanations of the lodgements and entries[89]. Furthermore, the Supreme Court had decided that "in order for a claim of debt outstanding in a customer's account with its Banker to succeed, the Bank must prove how the debit balance claimed from the Customer was arrived at....[90]" Section 6 thereof therefore effectively amends the Evidence Act, on the need for direct evidence as electronically generated statement of accounts can now be tendered I courts under the in evidence.

To entrench quicker recovery by the courts under the Failed Banks Act. Section 22 thereof states that the Act prevails over any other enactment or law in any case of inconsistency.

To secure the assets from jeopardy, the court may issue, an interim attachment of the debtor property under Section 3 of the Act and the court may also prohibit any disposition of the debtor's property, moveable or immoveable or to stop all outward payments, operations or transactions on the debtors account, based on prima facie case. The properties may also be vested in the court to preserve such assets pending the determination of the proceedings.

v. Application Process for Recovery of Debt

Procedurally, when a creditor issues a demand for settlement of a debt and the company fails to comply with the demand, the creditor has the right, without more, to petition for the winding up of the company[91]. For companies outside banks, the winding up process is deemed to have commenced once there is a resolution of member's voluntary winding up. A winding-up petition **under CAMA** is filed at the Federal High Court within the jurisdiction where the debtor company operates[92].

Under Section 7 of the Failed Banks Act "An application for the recovery of a debt owed a failed bank shall be brought before the court by the receiver or

---

[89] NDIC (Liquidator of all States Trust Bank) vs Plateau State Govt. & Ors, 1998, FHC/J/CS/75/204.
[90] Bilante International Ltd vs NDIC, 2011 15 NWLR (pt. 1270) 407 @428-429, paragraph E-b
[91] S. 408 CAMA
[9292] S. 251 of the Constitution of Federal Republic of Nigeria

liquidator of the failed bank and where there is no receiver or liquidator, by a person appointed by the Central Bank of Nigeria or the Nigerian Deposit Insurance Corporation".

The application must contain the following information:

(a) The name and address of the borrower,
(b) If the borrower is a body corporate, a partnership or a sole trader,
    (i) The address of its principal place of business,
    (ii) The names and addresses of its shareholders, directors, proprietors or partners, as the case may be;
(c) The amount of loan and advance outstanding;
(d) Details of securities pledged, if any; and
(e) Such other information as may be useful to the Court.

There is provision in the Act for a simple originating process in FORM A of the Appendix to the Schedule.[93] The Schedule is titled 'Procedure for the Recovery of Debts at the Federal High Court'. These are clear rules of procedure for proceedings under the Failed Banks Act. However, the Act and the Schedule do not specify the filing of an affidavit or pleadings in support of the application as required in general civil proceedings under the Federal High Court (Civil Procedure) Rules. Paragraph 3(5) of the Schedule thereof to the Act stipulates that the evidence need not be stated in the application.

Under section 8(1) of the Act and Paragraph 10(1) of the Schedule, the debtor is required to file a reply in response to the application. The form of the debtor's reply is not stated i.e. whether by way of an affidavit or by way of pleadings.

Furthermore, to ensure that actions are not extinguished due to laches or delay by parties, **Statute of limitation** of any state or that of the FCT is excluded from applying to matters brought before the court relating to debt recovery[94].

vi.   Summary Proceedings

For speedy recovery of loans, the Act and the Schedule provide for summary proceedings. The timelines for filing are shorter in that the debtor is to enter appearance not later than 15 days from the day of his service with the debt recovery application.[95] His reply to the application is expected to be filed within six (6) days after entering appearance.[96] Paragraph 22 of the Schedule to the Act also empowers the court to abridge the time upon an application. Day-to-day

---

[93] The Schedule is headed 'Procedure for the Recovery of Debts at the Federal High Court'. This operates as the Rules of Procedure for Proceedings conducted under the Failed Banks Act.
[94] S. 44 NDIC Act 2006
[95] Paragraph 5(2)
[96] Paragraph 10(1) FBA

hearing of debt recovery applications is also stipulated,[97] for speedy trial.

Where a debtor in his reply to the debt recovery application admits his indebtedness, the court will enter judgement for the admitted sum.[98] Under Section 8(2), therefore, the court may allow the debtor no more than 30 days within which to pay the admitted sum, but may proceed to the hearing of the debt recovery application where the debtor fails to pay the admitted sum within the time stipulated or where he disputes the debt. However, if the debtor pays the loan and interest within the period specified[99] under Sub-Section 8)2), the court shall issue the debtor a Certificate of Clearance and shall release to the debtor all documents and properties pledged as security for the loan. Under section 9(1)(a) thereof "where the debtor – having admitted the debt pursuant to section 8 – fails to pay the admitted sum within the time stipulated by the court, *"the Court shall proceed to hear the case and enter judgement and make such Orders as it deems appropriate for the purposes of this Part of the Act."*

Where the debtor disputes any loan or interest or fails to pay within the period prescribed under Section 8, the court shall proceed to hear the case and enter judgement or make any order it deems appropriate[100]. Also, the court may make an order for the payment of the loan and interests and if the debtor fails to pay within the specified period, the Court shall levy execution[101].

vii. The Evidence Required:

Section 1(3) of the Failed Banks Act mandates the court to conduct its proceedings in such manner as to avoid undue delay and all proceedings under the Act are to be held in open court. The Act dispenses with strict adherence to rules of evidence in the adjudication of matters which are brought thereunder.

The objective of this provision is to allow the court to focus on the merits of the claims rather than on procedure. A key provision of the Act is the power of the court to admit and act on any evidence which it considers relevant to the proceedings before it, notwithstanding that such evidence is inadmissible under any other law or enactment. Section 1(4) of the Act provides that:

> 'The Court shall have the power to admit and act on any evidence which it considers relevant in any civil or criminal proceedings notwithstanding that the evidence is inadmissible under any other law or enactment'.

Similarly, Section 22 of the Act provides that:

---

[97] Paragraph 17 of the Schedule
[98] Section 8(1) Failed Banks Act
[99] Section 8(3), FBA
[100] SECTION 9(1), FBA
[101] SECTION 9(2) FBA

'Where a provision of this Act is inconsistent with that of the Evidence Act or any other enactment or law, the provisions of this Act shall prevail and that other provisions shall, to the extent of its inconsistently, not be applicable.'

The implication of the above provisions is that the provisions of the Evidence Act are not binding on the Court in a debt recovery action under the Failed Banks Act. In the case of *NDIC V. Gateway Paper Products Ltd & Anor*[102], the court held that the provisions of the Act not only require the court to admit the evidence but also to act on it. Evidence may be rejected or regarded because of non-compliance with the Evidence Act or any other law as to evidence.

To simplify the evidential requirement in trial of cases under the Act. Section 6 of the Act allows examination reports by the Central Bank of Nigeria (CBN), the NDIC or any person appointed by either of the institutions as sufficient proof of the existence of a debt, meaning that the onus is on the customer to prove repayment of the loan or overdraft.

viii. Concurrency of Criminal and Civil proceedings

Section 7(3) of the Act allows a debt recovery application to be filed, notwithstanding the pendency of a criminal proceeding. This statutory rule recognises that *Rule in Smith v. Selwyn* is anachronistic and no longer applicable in Nigeria.[103] The rule provides that where a civil wrong is also a crime, a civil action cannot be brought before the court until the criminal matter is concluded or a cogent reason for default of criminal action is provided.

In the case of *Alao v. Nigerian Industrial Development Bank.*[104] The court of Appeal held that continued application of the Rule in *Smith v. Selwyn* will work injustice, in view of the nature and pace of criminal trials in Nigeria. Proof of a criminal matter is quite different from proof of a civil matter (in this case, for recovery of debt) and there was really no justifiable reason why the two should be related.

For speedy recovery of debts, Section 3 of the Act empowers the court, at any stage of the proceedings, where it finds that a prima facie case has been made out against a person, to make an Order attaching the person's properties and bank accounts pending the determination of the proceedings.

Interlocutory Orders may be made aimed at preserving assets from which a judgement debt may be settled in the event that judgement is entered against a

---

[102] (2018) LPELR-43795 (CA)
[103] (1914) 3 KB 98
[104] (1999) lpelr-6673(CA)

debtor. Nevertheless, such orders exert pressure on a debtor and compel early settlement of the debt or quick settlement plan.

Although, a director or a shareholder of a company is generally not liable for the indebtedness of the body corporate unless he gave a guarantee or stood surety for the debt,

ix.   Sale by Auction or Private Contract

For prompt and effective realisation of the subject assets, sale by auction or private contract is allowed under the Act. Once a property is sold under Section 11(1), the Court has the power to execute an instrument of transfer which is conclusive proof of title by the purchaser. The consent of the Governor as required by the Land Use Act is not required.

However, compliance with the following requirements must be made:

(i)   Monies recovered from the sale under section 11(1) are to be paid to the Liquidator or Receiver within two weeks from the date of sale.

(ii)   If the money recovered from the sale is insufficient to cover the judgement debt, further execution can be levied against the other assets of the individual or body corporate or against the personal assets of the directors, partners or individuals (in the case of an association).

b. The NDIC Act

Another relevant provision on bank recoveries is **Section 39 (1) of the Nigerian Deposit Insurance Corporation Act 2006 (NDIC Act)**[105]which empowers the NDIC, in consultation with the CBN, to form a bridge bank to assume the deposit and liabilities of any failed bank. The bridge bank, so incorporated, will be given a banking licence by the Central Bank of Nigeria to act and carry out activities like a regular bank[106]. Thus, the NDIC may utilise a bridge bank for liquidation purposes, or for restructuring. Where a systematically important bank (SIB) or a bank that is "Too Big to Fail" becomes insolvent and the CBN as a regulatory agency revokes its licence, the NDIC (usually through the special purpose vehicle of a bridge bank) may also completely liquidate the assets of the bank and dissolve it, or may assume control of the Bank and collaborate with AMCON to "save" the bank[107]. The failure of any big financial institution may trigger national disruption of the larger financial system and economic disorientation.

---

[105] *The NDIC Act, CAP N102 L.F.N. 2006*
[106] Federal Mortgage Bank of Nigeria v NDIC (Liquidator of United Commercial Bank Limited) in Liquidation, (1999) 2NWLR (Pt. 591) 3333.
[107] S. 5 Asset Management Corporation Act, 2010 (AMCON Act).

The special resolution of banks is based on section 40 of the NDIC Act. The NDIC recently became the provisional liquidator of Skye Bank now called Polaris Bank[108]. The bridge bank – Polaris Bank – was in turn sold to the Asset Management Corporation of Nigeria (AMCON) by the NDIC. The aim of the rescue process was to save depositors' funds and to ensure that the bank continued as a going concern, being a **"systemically important bank"**.

Any bank, whose licence has been revoked or withdrawn by the CBN, becomes a failed bank. By definition, a failed bank is an insured institution whose capital to risk, weighed asset ratio or regulatory capital falls below the minimum prescribed by the CBN[109]. On another hand, a bridge bank is defined as a financial institution that is authorised to hold the assets and liabilities of another bank, specifically an insolvent or failed bank[110]. A bridge bank is usually charged with the responsibility of continuing the operations of the insolvent/failed bank until the bank becomes solvent, acquired by another entity, or liquidated and totally dissolved.

c. AMCON Act

In the recovery of bank loans, the role of AMCON is crucial. The functions of AMCON include[111] the acquisition and disposition of eligible bank assets and equities in accordance with the provisions of the Act with the approval of the Central Bank of Nigeria[112]. After the acquisition, AMCON may recapitalise the Bridge bank by purchasing the bank through acquisition of a significant equity in the bank amounting to control which should reverse the bank's negative equity position. As an alternative, AMCON could source new investors in the bank.

Under **Section 5, 25 and 30 of the AMCON Act[113]**, AMCON can also purchase the assets of a bank referred to as an eligible financial institution [114] in collaboration with the Central Bank of Nigeria.

The assets referred to as eligible assets are assets of an eligible financial institution specified by the Governor of the Central Bank of Nigeria as being eligible for acquisition by the Corporation[115]. Assets include the "Financial Assets" of the Bank. The Asset Management Corporation Act (Amendment Act)[116] has included a new term called "eligible equity" which it defined as *"shares, stock or other interest in the equity or share capital of an eligible*

---

[108] **Section 40 (1) of the Nigerian Deposit Insurance Corporation Act (NDIC Act)** CAP. N102 L.F.N. 2004

[109] S. 37 NDIC Act

[110] S. 39 NDIC Act

[111] S. 5, AMCON Act.

[112] See *Federal Mortgage Bank of Nigeria v NDIC* (1999) 2NWLR (Pt.591) 333.

[113] *Federal Mortgage Bank of Nigeria v NDIC* (1999) 2NWLR (Pt.591) 333.

[114] Nigerian Deposit Insurance Act CAP. N102 L.F.N. 2004

[115] section 24 of the Act

[116] AMCON (Amendment Act), 2015

*financial institution",[117]*has been included as assets of the bank.

Section 61 of the AMCON Act, defines an eligible institution as a bank duly licensed by the Central Bank of Nigeria to carry on the business of banking in Nigeria under the BOFIA and shall include a bank or other financial institution, whose banking licence has been revoked by the Central Bank of Nigeria, pursuant to the Banks and Other Financial Institutions Act.

As in s. 417 CAMA, once winding up has commenced, any activity or action which purports to deprive the failed bank of its property, whether through sequestration, attachment or even execution of a judgement against the assets of the "Bank in liquidation" has no legal effect. Accordingly, where a creditor of a failed bank obtains a judgement, (but is yet to execute the said judgement against the bank) prior to the revocation of the bank's license, the judgement cannot subsequently be executed against the failed bank. Obviously, s**ection 414** of CAMA does not cover judgements concerning the estate of the company undergoing winding-up as where a mere declaratory judgement is given on behalf of a third party against the company. The only recourse open to the creditor is to present a claim to the liquidator, which will be treated according to priority ranking in liquidation of the affairs of the bank.

The effect of **Section 414 CAMA** is to immediately trigger the grant of a winding up order by the Federal High Court which initiates the winding-up process as opposed to being triggered by the appointment of a provisional liquidator. The question which arises is whether the judgement creditor upon notice of the appointment of a liquidator or the revocation of a bank license, can subsequently execute the judgement before winding up order is obtained by the provisional liquidator.

It is notable that both NDIC and BOFIA Acts confer the responsibility of obtaining a winding up order from the Federal High Court on the NDIC once the NDIC becomes the provisional liquidator of a failed bank[118].

d. BOFIA Act

Section 40 of BOFIA provides as follows; *"where the license of a bank has been revoked pursuant to section 39 of this Act, the Corporation shall apply to the Federal High Court for a winding up order of the affairs of the Bank[119]*.

Post-Judgement applications/Motions made against a Failed Bank: Any application made by the creditor after the license has been revoked and a provisional liquidator (NDIC) appointed will be considered as ancillary or consequential reliefs, and will not be subject to section 417 of CAMA.

---

[117] Section 61 AMCON (Amendment Act)
[118] Section 40 (2) of the Nigeria Deposit Insurance Act CAP. N102 L.F.N. 2004 and Section 40 of the Banks and Other Financial Institute Act 2007
[119] NDIC vs Alhaji Nasidi Mohammed & Ors. (2018) LPELR-44744 (CA).

Consequently, post judgement applications are not considered as "freshly instituted or constituted proceedings" as envisaged by Section 417[120]. This means that section 417 is only applicable to actions which are just about to be "freshly instituted or proceedings which are already pending in court" against a company for which a provisional liquidator has been appointed. Accordingly, section 417 would not apply in respect of matters which had already been concluded before the appointment of the provisional liquidator. In effect, Section 417 of CAMA does not extinguish the right of the failed bank to institute action against any other person[121].

Sections 414 and 417 of CAMA are part of the basic frameworks in creating and implementing an insolvency regime for failed banks with the objectives of protecting the entire depositors and creditors of failed banks in liquidation and ensuring the protection of creditors' rights and interest.

In addition to the oversight responsibilities of the CBN and the NDIC for financial stability, the Act provides that the Central Bank of Nigeria (CBN) may turn over the control and management of a failing bank to NDIC on terms and conditions [122]as the CBN may stipulate. Also, the Act provides that no suit shall be instituted against a bank whose control has been assumed by the Corporation. If any such proceeding is instituted in any court or tribunal against the bank, it shall abate, cease or be discontinued without further assurance other than this Act.[123]

One crucial provision of BOFIA is the setting aside of the general principle that a secured creditor has priority over an unsecured creditor. Thus, Section 54 of the BOFIA provides that *"where a bank is unable to meet its obligations, or suspends payment, the assets of the bank in the federation shall be available to* **meet all the deposit liabilities of the bank and such deposit liabilities shall have priority over all other liabilities of the bank.** Thus, priority ranking under the BOFIA is to the effect that depositors must have priority over other secured/unsecured creditors. This led to the case of *First Bank of Nigeria Plc. v. Nigeria Deposit Insurance Corporation[124].* The facts of the case are these: Prior to the revocation of Lead Merchant Bank's (LMB) licence, LMB was indebted to First Bank of Nigeria Plc.'s (FBN) under a clearing and settlement banking transaction. To this end, FBN secured its interest with an unregistered legal mortgage over LMB's property. However, upon liquidation of LMB by the Nigerian Deposit insurance Corporation (NDIC), FBN made repeated demands from NDIC for the payment of LMB's outstanding indebtedness to it.

[120] *Federal Mortgage Bank of Nigeria v NDIC (Liquidator of United Commercial Bank Limited) in Liquidation (1999) 2 NWLR Pt.591, 1999 21 Law SC. 66, 1997..*
[121] *Onwuchekwa vs NDIC* (2002) 5NWLR (PT. 760) 371 AT 393, **Agro Allied Development Ent. Ltd v MV Northern Reefer & Ors.** (2009) 12 NWLR (Pt. 1155) 255 S.C.
[122] Section 36 BOFIA Act
[123] Section 41 (1) & (2) BOFIA Act
[124] Federal High Court, 2017, Hon. Justice Ibrahim Buba (Punch Newspaper, 20th March, 2017).

In response to the demand, NDIC contended that whilst it recognised FBN's interest in the property of LMB, it must comply with priority ranking under the BOFIA in settling same, which is to the effect that depositors of LMB must have priority over all other secured/unsecured creditors. FBN's interest in the LMB's property was secured by an unregistered mortgage, which makes FBN essentially an unsecured creditor.

The learned trial judge dismissed the contention by FBN by relying on Section 54 of the BOFIA. The trial court reasoned that the right of the mortgagee to institute an action had not crystallised since all the depositors had not been paid.

i. The Justification for Priority of Bank Deposits in Nigeria

Based on the **Depositors Preference Rule i.e.** the claims of depositors enjoy a privileged status in the event of insolvency of a bank over secured and unsecured creditors.

The objective of the protection of depositor's fund is to maintain the assets of banks for the benefit of depositors, to minimise the negative consequences of bank runs. This rule is further reinforced by the fact that depositors are not only viewed as creditors of the bank but are also persons entitled to a claim for premiums charged on **insurable deposits** with the bank.

Section 2 of the NDIC Act[125] provides that: *"All deposits of a licensed bank or any other financial institution shall be insured with the Corporation."* This in effect entails that procedurally, the bank must be in compliance with its obligations to contribute to insurance of its deposits under Section 54 of the BOFIA as a pre-condition before the NDIC can realize the bank's interest[126]. *"if the Bank is unable to meet its obligation, or suspend payments, the assets of the bank in the Federation shall be available to meet the obligations of the bank and such deposit liabilities shall have priority over all other liabilities of the bank? The question is: What are the assets of the bank that are available to meet the obligations of the bank?* Ordinarily, the assets of the bank comprise owned or possessed assets and are limited to, *cash and balance at the Central Bank of Nigeria, treasury bills and other eligible bills, loans and advances to banks/customers, debt securities, equity shares (and other variable yield instruments), participating interest, tangible and intangible fixed assets, etc.* Hence, where a security interest is created that takes away the asset from the ownership of the bank, that asset cannot be said to belong to the bank for purposes of distributing it amongst its creditors.

---

[125] Cap 301 LFN 2004
[126] First Bank of Nigeria Plc. v Nigerian Deposit Insurance Corporation (Federal High Court) Punch Newspaper, 28/7/17.

e. Secured Transaction in Movable Assets Act, 2017

Another legislation on recovery of debt is the Secured Transaction in Movable Assets Act, 2017 which permits the taking of security over movable assets. In practice, the question arises whether a bank which has granted security over its movable assets is subject to Section 54 of the BOFIA due to the general principle that a charge is only an encumbrance, and the movable asset continues to remain with the bank.

The resolution of the issue then is by determining the proper definition of assets from the accountants view. The assets of the bank are equal to its liability plus its capital. Whereas the lawyer sees the assets of the bank as equal to net assets meaning that, the assets of the bank comprise ownership plus possession. So, where a security interest is created that takes away the asset from the ownership of the bank, then that asset cannot be said to belong to the bank for purposes of distribution amongst its creditors.

Legally, a charge does not necessarily transfer ownership to the chargee but is an equitable encumbrance on the asset. Unlike a mortgage, a charge does not give an immediate right to be paid from the charged property. A chargee must appoint a receiver or approach the court for an order to sell. This differentiation presents a situation where a mortgage created in certain parts of the country, operating the property and Conveyancing Act of 1881 and Property and Conveyancing Act like the old Western Region, Lagos etc. excludes the mortgaged asset from the assets of the bank and no longer available for distribution by the creditors.

On another hand, where a mortgage is created in the conveyancing states, such mortgage would be available for distribution to the creditors. Section 41 of BOFIA, provides that *"the Corporation liquidation expenses enjoy priority over all other liabilities **including over legal mortgage or crystallized debentures".***

3. Duties, Functions and Liabilities of directors/managers

Until wound up, the directors of banks and ailing companies continue to owe fiduciary and non-fiduciary duties to their companies such as duty of care and skill, to keep proper books of records, not to enter into transactions which may jeopardize the creditors funds, to observe the utmost good faith towards their companies in all transactions, and also not to indulge in fraudulent trading or under value transactions[127].

Particularly, the duties under section 279(7) (CAMA) state that, the directors/managers must not abdicate from their responsibilities or allow their

---

[127] S. 279(1) CAMA

personal interests to conflict with their duties[128]. They must not make secret profit or other benefits and must not misuse corporate information and property in their possession as the company still exists. Jointly, the Failed Banks Act, and CAMA, allow the courts to hold directors, shareholders, partners, managers, officers and other employees of failed banks who are connected to debts and loans to be jointly and severally liable where the security is impossible to locate or debtor is unlocated or non-existent, fake or fictitious. Both laws are complementary in the pursuit of creditor's protection, and state that a company becomes insolvent if it is indebted to its creditors in a sum exceeding N2, 000 and is unable to pay same after statutory notice demanding payment or to secure or compound the debt satisfaction[129].

CAMA's definition of an insolvent person is also unrealistic: any person in Nigeria who, in respect of any judgement, decree or court order against him, is unable to satisfy execution or other process issued thereon in favour of a creditor, and the execution or other process remains unsatisfied for not less than six weeks[130]. This definition implies that a court order may be made even in cases of clear balance sheet insolvency where the company's liabilities exceed the assets of the company. In practice, once a company's liabilities exceed the company's assets such a company is insolvent. For banks, the CBN's report on the financial health of a bank is sufficient proof of insolvency[131]. For failed banks, disposal of the Bank's property, movable or immovable, and all outward payment on debtors account must be halted. Consequently, once the company is insolvent, the directors' must consider the interest of creditors for priority over those of shareholders and the directors must seek to minimise losses and maximise value for creditors**[132]**.

Under CAMA, erring directors may be criminally liable for pre-insolvency acts such as inducing any person to give credit to the company by false pretences or fraud; making or causing any gift/transfer of a charge on the company's property or causing execution to be levied with the intent to defraud creditors; concealing or removing the company's property within two months before the date of a judgement/order for payment of money obtained against the company[133]. Directors will also be criminally liable if they trade recklessly or with intent to defraud creditors[134]. Directors, who misapply company funds, are liable to account for the company's money or property and may be compelled to repay with interest.[135]

---

[128] S. 280 CAMA
[129] Section 40 CAMA
[130] Section. 650 CAMA
[131] NDIC Act
[132] West Mercia Safetywear v Dodd , HLC Environmental projects v Carvalho. In Brady v Brady. (1987) 3 BCC 535 at 552
[133] Section 504 CAMA
[134] Section. 506.
[135] Section. 505 CAMA

4. **The legal position of unsecured creditors i.e. landlords, employees, trustees, other interested persons: The Pari-Passu Principle**

Under CAMA, the court is empowered to appoint a Receiver/Manager where a security is at risk based on an application[136]. The application may be made by the receiver members/shareholders, creditors, or representatives, trustees in bankruptcy, a contributory, or an interested person[137]. An application may be made to the court for the judicial sale of the company's assets in order to recover the debts, or for the appointment of a receiver in order to recover the debts of the company, for the principal debt and interest.

After judgement, repayment may be enforced on the moveable and immovable assets of the debtor through attachment of the movable or immovable property, garnishee proceedings, or judgment summons.

Further, there are provisions for preferential payment of all local rates and charges, due and payable, assessed taxes, pension fund contributions, wages and salaries, employee holiday remuneration etc.[138]. However, this priority ranking is in conflict with BOFIA which gives priority of liquidation expenses over all other liabilities including over legal mortgages or crystallised debentures[139]. Priority ranking under CAMA is therefore subject to the Failed Banks and the NDIC Act, for banks only. Priority ranking under CAMA will continue to apply outside failed banks.

5. **Voidable and Impeachable transactions**

Companies, who are distressed financially or who are unable to pay their debts as they fall due, are statutorily barred from embarking on new transactions unless their negative financial situation is positively reversed[140]. Such transactions by distressed organisations are usually termed fraudulent trading, misfeasance, undervalue transactions or wrongful trading. Fraudulent trading arises to defraud creditors, while misfeasance consists in the misuse of company's property; misapplication of company's funds consists in utilising company's resources for non-company purposes, or making illegal/unauthorized payments. Undervalue transactions consist in share transfers and transactions at undervalue, wrongful trading which involve obtaining credit on behalf of the company without any clear cut realistic prospect of repayment. Under Common Law and various statutes in Nigeria, there are remedies available like injunctions to prevent debtors from misusing assets or absconding, recovery of commission/interests, attachment of movable or immovable properties and

---

[136] Section. 409 CAMA
[137] Section. 409 CAMA
[138] Section. 494 CAMA
[139] Section 54 BOFIA & Section 20&21 NDIC Act
[140] CAMA, BOFIA and NDIC Act

appointment of Receiver/Manager[141].

Also, the veil of incorporation may be lifted to hold the directors and other errant officers personally liable for crime and civil breaches. Other remedies available include rescission of the transactions, damages, and criminal indictment and conviction[142].

However, to sustain the distressed company's operations, a receiver is empowered to borrow money on the security of the property in his possession, upon approval of the court. The creditor of such loan is protected to the extent of the claim having priority over debenture holders who initiated the appointment of the receiver.

6. Group Insolvency: Lifting the Corporate Veil of Incorporation:-

The issue of insolvency further becomes complex where the group or subsidiaries become insolvent due to various factors ranging from mismanagement, unprofitability, non-diversification, government regulatory requirements etc. Since it is a fundamental principle of law that an incorporated company is separate from its members, control by a company in a subsidiary does not translate to ownership and the separate entity of the subsidiary remains sacrosanct. [143]. Thus, the law maintains the veil of incorporation and the subsidiary company has its own separate legal personality, and the parent company is not ordinarily liable for the loans or acts of its subsidiary. [144] Accordingly, the subsidiary's assets and liabilities remain separate from those of its parent and affiliates, for the purposes of execution or for liability for debts of the other [145]. In this regard, section 567 of (CAMA) maintains separate definitions of "company" and "holding company". Under Part XV of CAMA, winding up proceedings apply only to companies not holding companies. Commencement of winding up proceedings for a company in a group, does not translate to automatic winding-up of other entities in the group. However, due to interlocking and interdependence of entities in a group, insolvency of an entity in a group, usually affects the solvency of the holding company. Where more entities in a group are insolvent, the proper procedure is to commence separate insolvency proceedings. Nevertheless, insolvency proceedings for insolvent affiliates in the group may trigger cross-default contract clauses of solvent affiliates. The liquidator would thereby need to enforce obligations against the solvent affiliates separately which may necessitate additional insolvency actions. The affiliates may be exposed to liabilities associated with insolvency

---

[141] Section. 506 CAMA
[142] Section. 279 (9) CAMA and section 49&50 BOFIA
[143] Salomon v Salomon (1897) 1 AC 22.
[144] FDB Financial Services Ltd. v. Adesola (2000)8 NWLR (Pt 668) 171 at 83H-184A.
[145] Adams v Cape Industries Plc. (1990) BCLC 479 at 513. Bank of Tokyo v Karoon (1987) AC 45 at 64F.

proceedings, such as fraudulent trading under sections 495 and 506(1) of CAMA. Normally, the creditors would have recourse to the solvent affiliates to pierce the corporate veil and hold the solvent affiliates as shadow directors for breach of contract, negligence, deceit etc.

Recently, in **Re Southard & Co Ltd**[146], Templeman LJ had succinctly depicted this scenario by stating that even where a subsidiary declined into insolvency, the parent and other subsidiaries may "prosper to the joy of the shareholders without any liability for the debts of the insolvent subsidiary."

An important Nigerian case on this cross default scenario is Ecobank Plc. /Honeywell Group Dispute is relevant[147]. Honeywell Group was stated to be insolvent. Honeywell's subsidiaries (Anchorage Leisure Ltd, Honeywell Flour Mills Plc. and Siloam Global Ltd) had obtained bank facilities from the defunct Oceanic Bank Plc. which Ecobank had acquired in 2011. Honeywell (on behalf of its subsidiaries), negotiated the settlement of the debt resulting in N3.5bn payment to Ecobank. Honeywell contended that N3.5bn had been agreed as full and final settlement of the debt while Ecobank claimed it was part-payment of the original N5bn debt. Following the dispute, Ecobank, at different times, filed separate winding-up petitions against the subsidiaries and affiliates. The Court decided that due to the original debts being separately owed by the three different companies in Honeywell Group, a single winding up proceeding against Honeywell was incompetent.

7. Recommendations
a. The rate of bank insolvencies and collapses raises a need for urgent reorientation of managerial efficiency and transparency in Nigeria. A most salient factor is that the essentials of effective corporate governance must be installed in all companies. Whistle blowing schemes should also be encouraged more in corporate management to pre-empt corporate collapses.
b. Considerable progress has been made on reducing the rigours of proceedings e.g on burden of proof, applications and summary processes and other procedural and evidential requirements. However, the numerous laws on this subject need to be harmonised into one composite legislation for ease of application.
c. There is need for better inter-agency cooperation to reduce to the barest minimum the number of cases and loans outstanding. These agencies are mainly regulatory and can have a one-stop establishment encompassing NDIC, CBN, AMCON, SEC.

---

[146] (1979) IWLR 1198
[147] Honeywell Flour Mills Plc (FHC/L/CP/1571/2015) and (FHC/L/CP/1689/2015), Soloam Global Services Ltd (FHC/L/CP/1572/2015), Anchorage Leisures Ltd (FHC/L/CP/1570/2015) and Honeywell (FHC/L/CP/1571/2015).

d. A special regime should also be provided for MSMEs, and women entrepreneurs under the law for access to funds without security as the present law is tailored to suit big time users and suppliers of capital.

Conclusions

a. Alternative Dispute Resolution Mechanisms in debt recovery processes, should be adopted in all facility agreements, to minimise litigation which is inimical to business development.
b. Automation of court proceedings and provision of ICT gadgets for judges should expedite debt recovery. The culture of Nigeria in terms of political instability and poverty necessitates stricter and faster enforcement of the laws in this arena to reduce the psycho-social losses to the economy.
c. Nigerian laws are silent over group insolvency proceedings. Consequently, companies in a group may voluntarily decide to appoint one insolvency officeholder to save costs and avoid multiplicity of processes. However, under the law, each entity in a group must be treated as a distinct entity for the purposes of insolvency proceedings. This will however continue to increase cost of insolvency proceedings.
d. Where insolvency proceedings are instituted against companies in a group, the actions must be separate and unconsolidated actions.
e. There is a plethora of legislations and institutions on recovery of bank loans in Nigeria. The underlying objectives remain the sustenance of funds for the national economy through protection of contractual rights of capital suppliers.
f. The statutes and case laws are complementary of each other. However, judicial intervention should be more dynamic as our legislative draftsmen still need skills updating in the unique sphere of recovery of bank loans.

EFFICACIOUS AND PRAGMATIC METHODS IN DEBT RECOVERY PROCESSES

Introduction:

In a developing economic system as we have, it is evident that lawyers are always intentional about quickest recovery of debts to earn their professional fees. Upon consultation of a lawyer, a Letter of Demand is initiated to the debtor, warning about dire consequences if payment is not received on or before a stipulated date (usually 7 days after the delivery of the letter). If the debtor is a Company, a Statutory Letter of Demand for winding up of the Company will be served on the Company and upon expiration of the statutory period (3 weeks), a winding up proceeding be commenced against the Company for the Court to appoint a receiver to liquidate and sell off the insolvent Company's assets.
A Letter of Demand will show the debtor your level of seriousness to recover the debt and serves as a pre-action notice for a debt recovery proceeding. The debtor may pay up or negotiate an installment payment once he hears from a lawyer.

The Court has the power to hear and determine an action for debt recovery and enforce payment against a recalcitrant debtor. A lawyer, acting on behalf of the creditor, will commence a debt recovery action and for damages for breach of contract. The lawyer may also bring an application for the preservation of the moveable and immoveable property of the debtor pending the final determination of the court proceedings. Where the debtor is a company, winding-up proceedings may be commenced along with the action for Summary Judgment against the debtor. It is trite law that in an action for the recovery of debt, the cause of action accrues upon demand for the payment of the debt. Where no demand is made, a cause of action does not arise and no action can be commenced in court. So until such a letter of demand is issued, no right of action would arise and accrue to enable commencement of legal action in a Court of law for the recovery of the debt in question. In the case of Hung v. E.C. Invest. Co. Nig. Ltd[148], this stance confirmed was that: – "In a claim for recovery of a debt, the cause of action accrues when a demand is made and the debtor refuses to pay." A letter of demand serves as a pre-action notice for a debt recovery proceeding. The debtor may pay up or negotiate an instalmental payment once he or she has received a demand notice.

---

[148]

The initiation of a debt recovery process generally depends on the nature of default and the response of the debtor. Accordingly, the following practical steps may be used:

1. **Issue a reminder**: This is the first step a creditor should adhere to. Thus, the creditor is to send a reminder through written letters, mails or SMS reminding the debtor of his failure to pay the debt as and at when due and the importance of doing so as refusal may make the creditor to institute the matter in court. Where the debtor does not make payment after the reminder, a further mail to the debtor, referring to the reminder earlier sent should be made. The letter of reminder can be drafted by the creditor or through his lawyer.

2. **Negotiate on new terms of payment**: It is important for the creditor to give room for discussion and negotiate with the debtor on new terms of payment of the debt where it is glaring that the debtor is desirous of paying the debt but for circumstances beyond his/her control, was unable to do so at the actual date fixed for paying the debt. Thus, payment in installments, a new date for the payment of the debt or selling of valuable goods or property of the debtor to settle the debt could be used as a form of paying up the debt owed.

3. **Fall back to the agreement earlier made**: Where the parties have made an agreement before the loan, goods or services were given out, it is important for the creditor to fall back on the said agreement to know if an alternative method of resolving the problem before going to court should default be made in paying the debt, was stated therein. Where such is the case, the creditor should first follow such method before going to court.

4. **Letter of demand:** A letter of demand can be issued to the debtor(s) stating the debt owed, the date which such loan, goods or services were given out, the agreed date it ought to have been paid and the deadline stating that the creditor will commence an action in court where the debt remains unpaid. This letter is an evidence that the creditor has in fact notified the debtor of the debt owed and such payment has not been made. The letter can be drafted by the Creditor's lawyer. Hence the need for the creditor(s) to employ the services of a lawyer.

   In the case of Unity Bank v Olatunji[149], the appellant instructed the respondent's law firm to take necessary measures to recover a specified amount owed by debtors of the appellant. The letter of instruction provided that the respondent's fee was "10 percent of the amount recovered". The respondent instituted an action against the appellant's debtors and judgment was given against the debtors for the payment of the debt on 26 October 2008. The debtors thereafter filed an application and obtained an order for instalmental payments. The appellant terminated the respondent's brief on 23 October 2008 and the respondent

---

[149] (2016) LCN/830 (CA)

filed an action for 10 percent of the balance of the total (judgment) debt yet to be paid.

In a similar case, of *Savanah Bank v Opanubi* (supra) neither the court nor counsel in *Olatunji* made reference to the Supreme Court decision. The appellant instructed the respondent (a legal practitioner) to recover about N99.3m owed to the appellant by a debtor. The letter of instruction stated that the respondent's fee would be 10 percent of the actual amount recovered by the respondent. The respondent filed an action against the debtor resulting in a judgement in terms of the claim. The debtor paid N50m out of the judgement debt from which the respondent was paid N5m. The appellant thereafter terminated the brief and afterwards received a further payment of N47.5m from the Central Bank of Nigeria on behalf of the debtor.

Although the Supreme Court held that the debriefing of the respondent constituted a breach of contract, the action failed on the ground that the respondent's claim was defective. The respondent had alleged that his claim was based on a *quantum meruit*, however the reliefs which he sought and the averments in his statement of claim did not support a *quantum meruit* claim as the respondent gave no particulars or information in his bill of charges upon which the court could fairly assess his claim on a *quantum meruit* basis.

> The Court of Appeal held that the respondent was only entitled to 10 percent of the debt recovered (i.e., paid) prior to termination of the respondent's brief on 23 October 2008. The court noted that the letter of instruction clearly stated that the respondent was to be paid 10 percent of the "amount recovered". This phrase, according to their Lordships, was used in the past tense not in future tense, e.g., "amount to be recovered"; hence, the respondent was only entitled to the actual amount paid by the debtors during the lifespan of the brief. Their Lordships relied on the settled principle that parties are bound by terms of their agreement and neither the courts nor a party can unilaterally rewrite the same. Accordingly, where the words used in contractual documents are unambiguous, courts must give the operative words their simple and ordinary meaning.

5. **Procedure agreed on by both parties in their agreement**: It cannot be overemphasized that an agreement should always be drafted when parties are getting into any form of contract, especially when it involves payment from one party to the other. The parties are allowed to include how any obligation or resulting debt owed to another party can be enforced or recovered in their agreement upon a breach by either party. They may resort to using the procedure they have chosen to follow under the agreement, which may include arbitration or any other alternative dispute resolution. The parties may resort to using a neutral third party in

resolving the issues if stipulated in the agreement. It could be by way of mediation, which will involve bringing a mediator to help resolve the issues

6. **Apply Alternative Dispute Resolution Mechanism**: It is important for the creditor to explore other methods of dispute resolution before resorting to litigation. Hence, the need for the creditor to use the Alternative Dispute Resolution mechanism to tackle the issue at hand. Parties often times include the Alternative Dispute Resolution clause in their agreement as a means of solving any problem in case of default but where that is not the case, the creditor can still use this means in solving the issue at hand. The Alternative Dispute Resolution methods include Mediation, Conciliation, Negotiation and Arbitration etc.

7. **Summary Judgment**: This is a fast approach to recovering the indebtedness of a person or entity especially when the debt is undisputed or has been admitted by the writing of letters or issuance of cheques or other forms of communication. As the name goes, "summary judgment" is a judgment obtained summarily, without going through the rigours of a full trial. In some Nigerian jurisdictions like Lagos, it is provided for under Order 13 of the High Court of Lagos State {Civil Procedure} Rules 2019, whereas in Abuja it is provided for under Order 11 of the High Court of the Federal Capital Territory {Civil Procedure} Rules 2018, and Order 35 of the High Court of the Federal Capital Territory {Civil Procedure} Rules 2018, which also provides for actions in the "undefended list. It should be noted that the sum being claimed must be liquidated money demand {that is the sum must be arithmetically ascertainable and precise}. The Creditor must also have the belief that the Debtor has no defense to the sum being claimed. To arrive at this belief that the Debtor has no defense to the claim, he is expected to furnish the Court with some relevant documents which will aid in proving the liquidated sum.

The documents are: Contract documents such as loan offer letters, duly executed deeds of guaranty and indemnity {where suing the guarantor of the loan} from which the claim or debt arose Statement of account or other instruments like receipts, invoices, vouchers, tellers establishing the debt that is being claimed Letters of demand from the Creditor and letters from the Debtor showing admission of some debt or obligation on the part of the Debtor, Once the above conditions and criteria are met, then the applicant can proceed with the summary judgment procedure or the undefended list procedure to recover the indebtedness of the Debtor. Once judgment is obtained, the Creditor can enforce the judgment against the Debtor, without further delay.

8. Enforcement under Convention on the Recognition and Enforcement of Foreign Arbitral Awards (New York Convention)

Nigeria is a signatory to the New York Convention on the Recognition and Enforcement of Foreign Arbitral Award 1958. Hence, the convention applies in Nigeria. Section 54 of the Arbitration and Conciliation Act 1990 domesticates the convention. Nigeria has a reciprocal obligation under the convention to recognise and enforce arbitral award granted in other co-signatory states.

9. Instituting an action upon the award

A plaintiff can bring an action upon the award in a Nigerian court and it would have effect as the judgement of the court. The plaintiff will need to establish that:

i. there is an existence of arbitration clause in the agreement;
ii. the arbitration was properly conducted in compliance with the agreement; and the award is valid.

A defendant may be left to challenge the award, the conduct of the arbitration or the jurisdiction of the arbitral tribunal.

1. Enforcement under the International Centre for Settlement of Investment Disputes (ICSID)

Nigeria domesticated International Centre for Settlement of Investment Disputes (Enforcement of Awards) Act on 29th November, 1967 for enforcement of awards given by ICSID. The ISCID Act allows for the recognition and enforcement of arbitral awards granted by ICSID.

A copy of the award duly certified by the Secretary-General of the Centre is deposited with the Supreme Court by the party seeking its recognition and shall be enforced like a judgement of the Apex court.

CONCLUSIONS AND RECOMMENDATION

i. Debt collectors, creditors and insolvency lawyers should be enlightened and trained on the debt recovery processes.
ii. Creditors should incorporate the process chosen in the debt instrumentse.g loan agreement, which should be well worded. Lawyers who are versed in insolvency matters must word such instruments efficiently.
iii. All parties must recognize the pivotal essence of business continuity and ensure optimum use of alternative and non-adversarial options.
iv. The Rule of Law must be adhered to at all times e,g Audi AlteramPartem, equality of parties before the law, independence of the judiciary and proof of the debt.

ENFORCEMENT OF DOMESTIC
AWARDS IN NIGERIA

1. Types of securities
i. Fixed and Floating Charges:

Sometimes, corporate borrowers deposited post-dated blank cheques for loans. The banks rely on s. 1(b) Dishonoured cheques (offence) Act (1977 (DCA)) which makes it criminal if a cheque presented within 3 months is unpaid due to insufficient funds and the defaulting debtors will be guilty of an offence punishable with conviction and/imprisonment.

The advantages of a floating charge for lenders, like financial institutions, were explained by Lord Millett in *Agnew v IRC (Re Brumark)*[150]. *Viz:*

> "The floating charge is capable of affording the creditor, by a single instrument, an effective and comprehensive security upon the entire undertaking of the debtor company and its assets from time to time, while at the same time allowing the company freedom to deal with its assets and pay its trade creditors in the ordinary course of business without reference to the holder of the charge."

Characteristically, the nature of a charge does not necessarily depend on the intentions or language of parties. Sometimes parties describe a fixed charge as a floating charge or otherwise. Thus, Millet LJ clarified that, "their ill-chosen language must yield to the substance'.

Furthermore, Mortgage Transactions, it must be acknowledged that a mortgage is that it is a conveyance or other disposition of land to secure the payment of money or the discharge of some other obligations.

Mortgagors are entitled to Equity of Redemption and Equitable Right to Redeem:

Often, mortgagors exercise the Equity of Redemption which is the right of a defaulting mortgagor to recover his property before a foreclosure sale by paying the principal interest and other costs that are due. This right of the defaulting mortgagor to reimburse the mortgagee and cure the default persists until the foreclosure sale.

---

[150] (2001) UK 28

In the case of *Oriorio v Igbinovia,*[151] the Court of Appeal relying on the Supreme Court decision in *Ejikeme v Okonkwo*[152] defined equity of redemption as *"An incidental right of every mortgagor to redeem the property mortgaged, which right is so inseparable from a mortgage that it cannot be taken away by an expressed agreement of the parties, that the mortage is not to be redeemable or that the right is to be confined to a particular description of persons*[153].

In *Anambra State Housing Development Corporation v Emekwe*[154] the Supreme Court held that an allottee of the appellant corporation could be regarded as a mortgagor entitled to retain his equity of redemption even after the contractual date of payment had passed. This equitable principle enures to the borrower to have a final opportunity to keep his or her property even if he or she has failed to make payments on the mortgage, until the property is sold in foreclosure proceedings.

The maxim is once a mortgage[155], always a mortgage,[156] as the right to redeem a mortgaged property is inseparable by express or implied from the incident of mortgage.

Final Remedies of a legal Mortgage

The legal mortgagee is entitled to several remedies following default by the mortgagor to repay not only the principal sum but also the interest.

The remedies are called final remedies because when successfully exercised by the mortgagee they operate to bring the mortgage to an end by discharging all the rights of a mortgagor free from the mortgage.

a. Foreclosure: This is the process where the court orders at the suit of the mortgagee or his successor-in-title that the mortgagor shall convey the land to the mortgagee unconditionally and free from any right to redeem.[157] It is immaterial that the mortgage was made merely by deposit of title deeds,[158] or was accompanied by a written memorandum.[159] The right to foreclosure flows from an order of court rather than self-help.

However, Section 51 of the Land Use Act defines *"a holder of right of occupancy"* Thus, a mortagagor is excluded and unless the law is amended, could militate against enforcement of his final remedies of sale

---

[151] (1998) 12NWLR (PT. 582) p. 426 at pp 441-442
[152] (1994) 8NWLR (pt. 362) p. 266
[153] Id at p.297
[154] (1996) 1NWLR (pt. 426)p. 505
[155] Ezekwesili v Agbapuonwu (2003)4SCNJ, Seton v Slade (1802) 7Ves 265
[156] Ndaba Nig. Ltd v UBN, 2007 NWLR pt. 1040 439. *Ejikeme v Okonkwo.*Sc 129/1989.
[157]James v James (1873) L.R. 16 Eq. 153.
[158] Backhouse v Chalton (1878) 8 Ch. 444
[159] York Union Banking Co. v Artley (1879) 11 Ch. D. 205; Carter v Wake (1877) 4 CH. D 605; Health v Push (1881) 6 Q.B.D. 345

or foreclosure of the mortgaged property. The mortgagee could proceed to recover his debt under an action for money had and received for which consideration has failed.

b. To Enter Upon and Take Possession of the Property

The mortgagee can enter upon and take possession of the mortgaged property from the moment the contract is concluded until the amount of the loan with the interest is received"[160]. In the case of *Nigerian Loan and Mortgage Co. Ltd v Aderunmobi[161]*, the defendant mortgaged a land which was leased to him for 99 years to the plaintiff company. The defendant wanted to use part of the loan to build a house in fulfilment of the covenant to that effect in the lease agreement. He neither built the house nor paid the interest due on the loan. In a purported exercise of their power of sale, the company put up the land for sale by auction. The plaintiff company eventually bought the land, entered into possession and began to erect a building thereon. Both parties then realised that a mortgagee could not sell the mortgaged property to himself without a court order.

c. An Action in Court

A legal mortgagee can have recourse to court demanding judicial assistance in recovering the loan as well as the interest. Proceedings could also be instituted under default summons or specially endorsed writs or under undefended list. These modes of commencing actions are used when there is demand for liquidated sum to achieve speedy recovery. The property of the mortgagor may be disposed of or attached or rfecovered by an action in 'Garnishee Proceedings.' All actions to recover the debt must be after the expiration of the date fixed for repayment.

d. Right of Sale

The legal mortgagee's remedy of sale of the mortgaged property was not so common as it is, currently. Thus, this remedy accounts for as much as about 70% of all remedies currently used by legal mortgagees in Nigeria. Most creditors, particularly financial institutions, require a clause granting power of sale in the event of default in the mortgaged deed. The purpose of sale is to help mortgagees recover the amount given out as loan as well as the interest[162]. To this effect, S. 123 of the Property and Conveyanacing Law 1959 grants the legal mortgagee the power to sell the mortgaged property without recourse to the

---

[160] Oluyode, op.cit at 465
[161] (1944) 17NWLR 136
[162] S. 19 Conveyancing Act 1881.

court. Once the mortgagor defaults, the power of sale arises and may be exercised on the occurrence of any one of the following conditions:

a. Notice in writing requiring payment of the mortgaged money, served on the mortgagor and default has been made in the payment of all or part of the loan for three months thereafter or;
b. Any interest under the mortgage is two months or more in arrears or
c. A breach of some other covenant in the mortgaged deed has been committed by the mortgagor.[163]

However, the provisions of Section 20 of the Conveyancing Act 1881 can be expressly excluded by providing in mortgage deeds that Section 20 of the Conveyancing and Law of Property Act 1881 shall not apply to this security and that the statutory power of sale shall be immediately exercisable by the mortagagee (usually a financial institution) or its assigns without the necessity of giving any notice in that behalf to the borrower at any time or times after the happening of any or either of the events specified hereof.

This type of clause in mortgage agreements seems like a subversion of due process created by provisions of the Property and Conveyanicng Law. Notably also, by virtue of section 125 of the Property and Conveyances Law of Oyo State, 1978, the mortgagor is protected by the provision that the mortgagee shall not exercise the power of sale conferred by law until a notice requiring payment of the mortgage money has been served on the mortgagor or one or two mortgagors and the defendant has defaulted in payment of the mortgage money or part thereof for three months after such service. Consequently, parties may still exclude the operation or waive the requirement of this provision or any notice at all in the mortgage deed without breaching the Law.

Sale of mortgaged property can be conducted by public auction or by private arrangement provided the sale was conducted bona fide. Any tinge of mala fides vitiates the sale. In *Ekaette v Nig. Housing Corporation*[164], *UBN Ltd v Professor Ozigi*[165], *Bank of the North Ltd v Alhaji Muri*[166], *Okonkwo v Commerce Bank*[167], the courts have consistently confirmed that the sale is unimpeachable even if a sale of a mortgaged property is conducted at an undervalue provided there is, good faith. As such, a mortgagee must act with reasonable care and must not be concerned with kindness or charity. But a sale to himself is invalid due to conflict of duty and interest. In *ACS Ltd v Ihekwoaba*[168].

---

[163] In Olori Motors v UBN (2006) 26 NSCOR 182.
[164] (1976) 6S.C. 183
[165] (1999) 2NWLR (pt.176)677
[166] (1998) 2NWLR (pt.536)153
[167] (2003) 2SCNJ 145
[168] (2004) FWLR pt. 194 at 570. Oluyode, Op.cit., at 475 and Mortgage Co. Ltd v Ajetunmobi (supra).

ii. Mortgages under the Land Use Act

Ordinarily, security for credit or mortgage transactions is valueless if it cannot be realised without difficulty when the need arises. A good security must, therefore, be readily ascertainable and stable over a fairly long period of time. It must also be easily transferable without undue cost and trouble to the mortgagees, including the ability of the mortgagee to obtain safe and indefeasible title with minimum trouble and delay; and without incurring residual obligation and liabilities to third parties in the process.

Mortgagees, especially banks and mortgage institutions have special preference for land as security for their credits resulting in the number of mortgages of land increasing in commercial importance. To enhance economic development, the ownership of all land in private citizens was extinguished and, or converted to a mere right of occupancy, following the nationalisation of land since 1978.

The validity of a mortgage under a statutory right of occupancy depends on whether, at the time of its creation, the consent of the Governor was sought and obtained.[169] The requirement of consent is indispensable to transactions under the statutory right of occupancy whether granted or deemed granted by the Governor.

The Legal Basis of Domestic awards on Debt Recovery

The Arbitration and Conciliation Act provides the legal framework for arbitration proceedings in Nigeria. According to Section 31 (3) of the Act, a party seeking to enforce a domestic award may, with the leave of the court, be enforced as a judgment or order of the court. The application to the court for enforcement and recognition of a domestic award is conveyed with a duly authenticated original award and arbitration agreement or a duly certified copy.

According to Order 39 Rule 4 of the High Court of Lagos State Civil Procedure Rules 2012, a party seeking to enforce or remit or set aside an arbitral award can do so with a motion on notice accompanied with an affidavit. Consequently, section 31 (2) of the Arbitration and Reconciliation Act and Order 39 Rule 4(2) provides that such application should be supported with the duly authenticated original award and arbitration agreement or the certified true copies. The award is enforced like a judgment of the Court.

Though the potency of a motion on notice has been questioned as an attempt by the High court to convert an arbitration award from a foreign country to its own

---

[169] Savannah Bank Ltd v Ajilo (1989) 1 NWLR (pt. 97) p. 305;

judgement, there is consensus is that an arbitral award has a similar status with a judgement of the court. **Ras Pal Gazi Construction Co. Ltd v F.C.D.A**[170]

A dissatisfied party with an award can apply to the court to set aside such award. However, the dissatisfied party has to show the court that the award contains decisions exceeding the scope of the issues submitted to the panel or outside the purview of the arbitration agreement.

2. Challenges in Debt Recovery Process

1. **Less Regulation in the debt Collection Industry**
   In Nigeria, there is no requirement for debt collectors to be licensed. This has made room for questionable characters and sharp practices in the debt collections industry in the country. There is an urgent growing need for Nigeria to regulate the business.
   Legally, apart from the Bankruptcy Act, general winding-up rules under the Companies and Allied Matters Act, and the recent Asset Management Corporation of Nigeria Act, there is no legislation regulating insolvency and debt collection in the private sector.

2. **Poor Record Keeping**
   Poor records keeping in Nigerian businesses and public registries alike makes tracking down debtors and resolving accounts difficult.
   Basic information like name, contact info and payment status may be inaccurate, and many registries still store information manually, making it a hassle to find important information. Additionally, there is no single record of the persons living in Nigeria.
   Some businesses have recently tried to institute training on record keeping. Also, the government is beginning to take steps towards new electronic record keeping methods, instead of manual ones. There remains a lot of work to be done.

3. **Inadequate public database**
   When a debt goes south, you want to be able to reach the debtor quickly. Most Nigerian cities are rapidly expanding and new residential areas are springing up without much municipal control. There are literally hundreds of new streets that are not reflected in any government municipal database, so finding someone at addresses provided becomes difficult. If the person moves to a new address, it becomes more cumbersome. There is no independent corroboration of any information provided by the registrant. This makes it tough to get infallible information about an

---

[170] **(2001) LPELR-SC.45/96**

absconding debtor's history from where a profile can be built which can be used to trace him. Also, the different government agencies in charge of public records maintain separate databases. The lack of a centralized public database makes it difficult to make a one-stop search to find anyone.

4. **Official secrecy and bureaucracy**

Getting information from government offices in Nigeria is like pulling teeth. The red tape involved is huge sometimes. It may take a Freedom of Information action to get information from government. No knowledge about or access to credit checks facilities. Most people would not give credit to customers if they knew such customers bad poor credit history. There are some credit bureaus in Nigeria but individuals do not have access to them except they are registered with the bureau. Again, most people do not know about them or that they can lodge complaints about unpaid debts to the bureaus.

5. Speed of litigation.

The court system in Nigeria is notoriously slow. A debtor with a bad defence but a good lawyer can delay your case in court for years with little or no penalties when judgment is eventually entered in your favour.

3. Recommendations & Conclusions

i. Financial institutions should undertake rigid application processes when requested for loans. They should ensure Credit checks and trade verifications should be strenuously with strict rules regarding accounts receivables.

ii. Creditors/Lenders should adopt measures that appear less aggressive and aimed at customers business continuity.

iii. Creditors should anticipate debtor excuses and have simpler debt collection process in place.

iv. Creditors should always consider foreclosure of secured properties at a last recourse and freeze accounts to recover whatever collaterals were provided.

v. Loan agreements ought to be carefully worded and documented preferably by lawyers.

vi. The banking sector should hire collection firms as they're more trained and experienced to conduct debt collection in a manner which will not affect the reputation of the bank and also not interfere with its operations.

vii.   Before instituting a matter in court for debt recovery, parties to loans should consider other amicable avenues as enumerated above to settle any issues at hand. Where the debtor, is adamant and refuses to pay up the debt then the court should be the creditor's last resort.

INTERLOCUTORY REMEDIES AND ARBITRATION ISSUES IN DEBT RECOVERY

Abstract

Lawyers, Creditors, debt collectors, and debtors alike are uncertain about how to pursue the process of debt collection. This study attempts to navigate the many options open to parties internationally and domestically.

The jurisdictions of local courts under municipal laws, conventions and case law have been re-examined and confirmed; to assist parties in the compass of their navigation of debt recovery. The role of arbitration has been examined in a milieu of protracted litigation, adversarial court processes and strained business relationahips and loss of financial resources.

The objective of their paper is mainly to adivise judicial officers, lawyers, creditors, law students to save the time of the courts.

As clarity has been provided, foreign direct investments would no lawyer be uncertain of what the courts will do to secure repayment of loans.

Keywords: Arbitration, Injunction, Court restrained order, Foreign Courts, Superior Court.

1. INTRODUCTION

Usually, the courts utilize various processes to enforce recovery of debts. The use of injunctions has been very effective in this regard.

However, there are different types of injunctions available by the Courts:

    a. Mareva Injunction
    b. Anton Pillar Injunction
    c. Exparte Interim Injuction
    d. Interlocutory Injunction
    e. Perpetual Injunction

i.   Mareva Injunction:

Under this injunction, the creditor could seize the property of his debtor before the judgment was delivered against the debtor and then retain the property as security for payment of the debt when he finally wins the case.

However, to remove the fears on the part of the creditor that maybe the debtor might dispose the properties prior to the judgment date, Mareva Injunction was introduced. Finally, the purpose of this injunction is to prevent the injustice of a defendant from taking away his assets which might be used in satisfying a judgment from the jurisdiction

However, the limitation of Mareva injuction are;

    a. It is not granted to enhance the position of the creditor as against other creditors by giving him priority on the assets of the debtors.

    b. It permits all drawings relating to the debtor's reasonable living expenses not more than a specific sum

    c. It does not spread to assets outside jurisdiction.

ii.   The Anton Piller order:

This is an order of court, made ex-parte and requiring a defendant or respondent to allow certain persons to enter his premises to search for documents and movable articles as are specified in the court order, and to permit such documents or articles to be taken away. It is seen as an Order of the Court that gives right to search premises and seize evidences without prior warnings. It is also called search orders.

iii.   An interlocutory injunction:

This is a court order to compel or prevent a party from doing certain acts pending the final determination of the case. It is an order made at an interim stage during the trial, and is usually issued to maintain the status quo until judgment is made

iv.   A Perpetual Injunction:

This is one ordered by the Courts to restrain any person from a judicial proceeding pending at the institution of the suit in which the injunction is sought, unless such restraint is necessary to prevent multiplicity of judicial cases. Ordinarily, it should be issued when the lawsuit underlying activity is resolved.

2. ENFORCEMENT OF ARBITRAL AWARDS FOR DEBT RECOVERY

In the age of globalization, increasing commercial transactions and trade is not without disputes. To guarantee a fair playing ground and the continuity of tranquil market space, it is commonplace to find dispute resolution clauses inserted into agreement between parties, especially when it involves multinationals. In the event of breach of the agreement, the dispute resolution clause defines the path the parties will chart in resolving their dispute.

Arbitration has emerged as a popular and effective mechanism for resolving commercial and trade disputes. Arbitration is favourable to parties because of its neutrality, confidentiality, speed, flexibility and the awards are easily enforced. The Supreme Court has held on the effect of arbitral award that "It is very clear and without any iota of doubt, that an arbitral award made by an arbitrator to whom a voluntary submission was made by the parties to the arbitration, is binding between the parties".[171]

An Arbitral award granted outside Nigeria is enforceable and binding on parties to it. A seamless ecosystem for enforcement of foreign judgments or arbitral awards boostS investors' confidence. According to World Bank Ease of Doing Business Index, 2018, Nigeria ranked 96th on enforcement of contract index and it takes about 454 days to enforce a contract through the court. The length and stress involved hurts business interest. Consequently, it is imperative that the arbitral award be enforced and respected in a seamless fashion.

3. ENFORCEMENT OF AWARDS GRANTED OUTSIDE NIGERIA
i.   Registration of the Award under the Foreign Judgments (Reciprocal Enforcement) Act 1990

The Act allows the enforcement and recognition of foreign judgements within six years of the judgement. The purport of the law is to accord recognition and enforcement to judgement of foreign courts that accords reciprocal respect to judgements of the Nigerian court.

Section 2 of the Act defines judgement to include arbitral award. Such judgment or award would have to be registered in a Nigerian court with the jurisdiction to hear the dispute. The judgment must be final and conclusive between the parties. The court will enforce monetary award payable and not fine or penalty.

The Federal High Court Civil Procedure Rules 2009 provides for the enforcement of foreign Arbitral awards. Order 52 Rule 17 stipulates that "where an award is made in proceedings on an arbitration in a foreign territory to which the Foreign Judgments (Reciprocal Enforcement) Act extends, if the award was in pursuance of the law in force in the place where it was made; it shall become enforceable in the same manner as a Judgment given by a court in the place and the proceedings of the Foreign Judgments (Reciprocal Enforcement) Act shall apply in relation to the award as it applies in relation to a Judgment given by that court."

---

[171] **Ras Pal Gazi Construction Co. Ltd v F.C.D.A (2001) LPELR-SC.45/96**

The Supreme Court in the case of **Macaulay v R.Z.B of Austria** has held that only judgments from superior courts in the United Kingdom and other commonwealth countries t are recognised and enforced in Nigeria[172].

ii.   Under Section 51 of the Arbitration & Conciliation Act,1990

Section 51 of the Arbitration and Conciliation Act guarantees the recognition of an arbitral award regardless of the jurisdiction it was granted and binding on the parties to it.

The party seeking to enforce the Award shall apply to the court. According to Section 32 of the Act, the party relying on an award or applying for its enforcement shall supply the court with:

a. a duly authenticated original award or a duly certified copy;
b. copy of the original arbitration agreement or a duly certified copy;
c. a duly certified translation in the English language if the award was not granted in English language.

In addition, Section 52 of the Act itemises the list of grounds for refusing recognition or enforcement.

iii.   Enforcement under Convention on the Recognition and Enforcement of Foreign Arbitral Awards (New York Convention)
Nigeria is a signatory to the New York Convention on the Recognition and Enforcement of Foreign Arbitral Award 1958. Hence, the convention applies in Nigeria. Section 54 of the Arbitration and Conciliation Act 1990 domesticates the convention. Nigeria has a reciprocal obligation under the convention to recognise and enforce arbitral award granted in other co-signatory states.
iv.   Instituting an action upon the award

A plaintiff can bring an action upon the award in a Nigerian court and it would have effect as the judgement of the court. The plaintiff will need to establish that:

a. there is an existence of arbitration clause in the agreement;
b. the arbitration was properly conducted in compliance with the agreement; and the award is valid.

A defendant may be left to challenge the award, the conduct of the arbitration or the jurisdiction of the arbitral tribunal.

---

[172] (2003) 18 NWLR (Pt. 852) 282

v.   Enforcement under the International Centre for Settlement of Investment Disputes (ICSID)

Nigeria domesticated International Centre for Settlement of Investment Disputes (Enforcement of Awards) Act on 29th November, 1967 for enforcement of awards given by ICSID. The ISCID Act allows for the recognition and enforcement of arbitral awards granted by ICSID.

A copy of the award duly certified by the Secretary-General of the Centre is deposited with the Supreme Court by the party seeking its recognition and shall be enforced like a judgement of the Apex court.

4. Conclusions and Recommendations

i.   There is a plethora of both domestic and international laws governing the enforcement of arbitral awards in Nigeria. Lawyers should endeavor to utilize these processes for efficacious recovery of debts.
ii.   The clarity in the Judicial processes aids foreign investors to access justice and engenders protection of foreign investments.
iii.   The Courts need to augment the initiatives made for arbitration to create a platform for economic and social development through speedy trials and compliance with the rule of law all through the process.

ENFORCEMENT OF JUDGMENT AND TRANS JURISDICTIONAL ISSUES IN DEBT RECOVERY MATTERS

ABSTRACT

The paper "Enforcement of Judgment in Debt Recovery Matters" is a research study into the often-complex questions that arise in the process of Debt Recovery in Nigeria today. The study is contemporary because the nation's banks now have a huge number of non-performing loans, many of which can be traced to unscrupulous businessmen and outright fraud. Jurisdictional Issues in Debt Recovery Matters" start by presenting a detailed explanation of the various methods of debt recovery available in Nigeria. These include the Writ of Fifa, Write of Sequestration, Garnishee Proceedings etc. Finally, typical issues and jurisdictional scenarios involved in debt recovery. The timeframe for judgement and grounds for refusing registration of judgement have been x-rayed.

INTRODUCTION:

Usually, receivers, liquidators, individuals and their lawyers are confused or uncertain as to which Court of record has the requisite jurisdiction to entertain any cause of action.

Section 251 (1) (d) of the Constitution of the Federal Republic of Nigeria, 1999 provides that both Federal High Courts and the State High Courts have the power to settle disputes between an individual customer and his bank. In effect, both Federal High Courts and the State High Courts have concurrent jurisdiction over Banker/Customer Relationship issues and transactions between a bank and individual customer.

In the case of UNIVERSITY OF CALABAR V AMCON & ORS[173], it was stated that the 3rd party notice served on the Appellant was in respect of the simple contract between the 2nd - 4th respondents and the Appellant and the other (University) respondents. It's not in dispute that the AMCON Act confers power on Federal High Court to hear recovery of debts. The 3rd party notice proceedings is between the Appellant and the 2nd - 4th respondents who is also

---

[173](2019) LPELR-47309 (CA). See BANK OF IRELAND v UBN & ANOR (1998) LPELR - 744(SC)

claiming recovery of debts flowing from the contract for which funds were taken from Union Bank Plc. to perform. Therefore, in the course of recovering debt it would be fatal and a rape of justice not to allow the debtor who says my money is in the hands of another. In fact, the very nature of third party notice procedure is to avoid multiplicity of actions and shorten litigation time. On the object of third party proceedings; "(i) that it is premature to raise objection to its liability albeit that the contention that it had entered appearance and so was bound in the third party procedure, is invalid and not sustainable. (ii) The objects of third party procedure or notice being aimed at preventing multiplicity of proceedings and the possibility of the same questions being litigated twice.[174] It is best to settle all matters in controversy once and for all. It ought to be noted, in addition, that the procedure applies not only to cases of contribution and indemnity but also to cases where any relief or remedy claimed by the defendant relates to or is connected with the original subject matter of the action and is substantially the same as some relief or remedy claimed by the plaintiff and to cases where any question or issue which relates to or is connected with the original subject matter of the action, should be determined not only as between the plaintiff and the defendant but as between either or both of them and the third party.[175] The need to make the 3rd party a party to the proceedings is the overriding need for the third party to be bound by the ultimate result of the action and the questions to be settled or resolved are prime considerations vide Peenok Investment Ltd. v. Hotel Presidential Ltd.[176] Besides, the provisions of Order 11 Bendel State (Civil Procedure) Rules, 1988 (ibid) allow for third party procedure in Rules 12(1) and (2) (in pari materia with the English RSC Order 16) are relevant and applicable as follows: "(1) Where in any action a defendant claims against any person not already a party to the action (in this section called 'the third party') (a) that he is entitled to contribution or indemnity; or (b) that he is entitled to any relief or remedy relating to or connected with the original subject- matter of the action and substantially the same as some relief or remedy claimed by the plaintiff; or (c) that any question or issue relating to or connected with the said subject-matter is substantially the same as some question on the issue arising between the plaintiff and the defendant and should properly be determined not only as between the plaintiff and defendant and the third party or between either of them; the Court or Judge in chambers may give leave to the defendant to issue and serve a third party notice. (2) The Court or judge in chambers may give leave to issue and serve a third party notice on an ex parte application supported by an affidavit, or where the Court or judge in chambers directs a summons to the plaintiff to be issued upon the hearing of the summons: provided that leave shall not be granted in cases where the action was begun and an order for pleadings made before the date of the commencement of these

---

[174]Standard Securities Ltd. v. Hubbard (1967) Ch. 1056 at 1059

[175]Chatsworth Investment Ltd. v. Amoco (U.K.) Ltd. (1968) Ch. 665, C.A. (iii)

[176](1982) 12 S.C.1; Green v. Green (1987) 3 NWLR (Pt.61) 480; Odu'a Investment Co. Ltd. v. Talabi (1991) 1 NWLR (Pt.170) 761 and Governor of Oyo State v. Folayan (1995) 8 NWLR (Pt. 413) 292. (iv)

rules."[177] There is no dispute on the contract and that its debts have not been settled, it's simply asking AMCON to collect the debt and convert it to what the 2nd - 4th respondents owe it, this then becomes an ancillary claim which the Court must determine.[178]

It is the writ and claim that selects the jurisdiction of a Court, in this case the introduction of AMCON has selected by statue to be Federal High Court, and therefore, it will defeat the purpose of 3rd party notice to hold otherwise. Therefore, the simple contract cases cited are not applicable herein, this is not a straight forward simple contract case, it's a relief connected with the debt recovery which by Section 53 of AMCON is within the context of Section 251 (1) of the 1999 Constitution (as amended)."[179]

Also, in FUTO OWERRI V AMCON[180]"Unarguably, the exclusive jurisdiction of the Federal High Court, are clearly enumerated in Section 251(1) of the Constitution of the Federal Republic of Nigeria, 1999 (as amended). Therefore, the jurisdictional extent of the Federal High Court does not extend to simple contracts or tort. [181] However, the Federal High Court, has the additional jurisdiction to entertain and determine any other matter as may "in addition be conferred on it, by an Act of the National Assembly." One of such Acts of the National Assembly is the Asset Management Corporation of Nigeria (AMCON) Act, Cap A24 A, 2010, (as amended). Section 53 of the aforementioned AMCON Act, donated the requisite jurisdiction of the Federal High Court to hear and determine matters relating to debt recovery, as shown in paragraph 28 of the 1st Respondent's statement of claim. And for the purpose of the instant case, the objects of the third party Rule/Proceedings were activated, in order to prevent multiplicity of actions and to enable the Court to settle the disputes between all the parties connected to the dispute, that is, the plaintiff, defendant(s) and the third party. This is to prevent the subject matter of the claim from being tried twice. Bank of Ireland y. Union Bank of Nigeria Limited & Anor.[182]

3.3 DEBT RECOVERY PROCESSES

It is a known fact that any judgment obtained in a court will be unproductive without the means of enforcing the judgment. Consequently, the major ways of executing a judgment in relation to debt recovery are:

> ➢ Writ of Fifa
> ➢ Attachment and Sale of Immovable Property

---

[177]Bullen and Leake and Jacob's Precedents of Pleadings, Twelfth Edition by I.H. Jacobs at page 1365." per ONU, J.S.C (PP. 23-25, PARAS. A-C).
[178]MERILL GURANTY SAVINGS & LOANS LTD v WORLD (Supra)
[179]*Per **OBASEKI-ADEJUMO, JCA** (Pp. 15-19, paras. B-C)*
[180](2019) LPELR-47327
[181]Opia V. Independent National Electoral Commission & Anor (2014) LPELR-22185 (SC); Odutola V. University of Ilorin 18 NWLR (Pt 1156) 563 et 462.
[182](1998) LPELR-744 (SC) page 16, paragraphs B-C. *Per **YAKUBU, JCA** (Pp. 40-41, paras. E-F)*

- ➢ Writ against goods and chattel
- ➢ Writ of Sequestration Garnishee Proceedings
- ➢ Winding Up Proceedings

WRIT OF FIFA

This is also known as Writ of Fieri Facias and it is the most popular form of enforcement of payment of judgment debts. However, the effect of this writ is the attachment and sale of the judgment debtor's property to realize the judgment debt. Furthermore, in a situation where a court has made an order for payment of the judgment debt by installments, then the order operates as a stay of execution of the judgment and afterward the writ may be issued only for the amount of installments which have become due on such default.

The Effect of Writ of Fifa:

This process of execution of judgment binds the property in the hands of the execution debtor, starting from the time when the writ is delivered to the sheriffs to be executed and that for the better expression of such time, when it will be the duty of the security without fee, as at the time of receiving such writ and to endorse on the back of the writ the hour, day, month and year when he received the writ. Writ of Fifa is issued on an application of the judgment creditor or his lawyer by filing of a precipe in the prescribed form and this will be accurately completed and all the feds will be paid.

WRIT AGAINST GOODS AND CHATTEL

This is the duty of the Sheriff, who has the deputy sheriff and the Bailiffs to support him. It is the Legal officer that carries out the seizing and sale of the goods. However, the Legal officer is the agent of the Sheriff and not the execution creditor. Also, the registrar will forward the writ to the Sheriff or Deputy Sheriff of the area where the execution is to take place

SALE OF ATTACHED MOVEABLE PROPERTY

In this case, the sale of the debtor's properties will be by public auction except where on application, the court orders selling of the goods privately. However, private selling without leave of court but with the agreement of the debtor remains legitimate unless on application the court can set it aside. More so, no goods seized in execution under process of a court must be sold because of satisfying the writ of execution until the expiration of a period of at least five days after the goods have been seized except the goods are perishable in nature or the owner of the goods that is being seized make such requests in writing.

WRIT OF SEQUESTRATION

A writ of sequestration is directed against the property of the judgment debtor in relation to both movable and immovable property. It results in vesting all the property in the possession of the sheriff and this prevents the debtor from making use of the property. If the property is merchandise, the debtors cannot sell and if it is housing property, the debtor cannot enter them or receive any rents or profit due to him on the property. However, order 11 of 9 Judgment Enforcement makes a provision that "a writ of sequestration shall be directed to two or more commissioners to be appointed by the court. Thus, they shall be commanded and given authority to enter upon all the immovable property of the person against which the writ has been issued.

The Effect of Writ of Sequestration:

This writ binds real property and personal property in possession from the time it has been issued. Furthermore, where sequestration of a contemnors' assets has been ordered, whoever knowingly takes any action that tends to prevent the sequestrator from carrying out his duty will be seen as obstructing a court order and therefore technically in disrespect of court.

GARNISHEE PROCEEDINGS

This is a mode of execution in which a debt that is due to the judgment debtor from another person is attached by the judgment creditor in order to satisfy the judgment debt and costs. Furthermore, this is a useful attachment of the debtor's effects in the garnishee's hands and is a form of execution of a judgment which is given by court against the debtor. More so, the parties to the garnishee proceedings are: Judgment debtor, Judgment creditor and debtor to the judgment debtor.

WINDING UP PROCEEDINGS

This is a statutory process of dissolution of a company. It is a process whereby the operations of a company are brought to an end and its assets are sold and the proceeds will be distributed to those whom the company is owing.

4.1 ENFORCEMENT OF FOREIGN JUDGMENTS

Foreign judgments, may in certain cases, be recognized and enforced in Nigeria and judgment in Nigeria can also be enforced in other countries. The act that makes provision for the enforcement of foreign judgments in Nigeria is the Foreign Judgments (Reciprocal Enforcement) Act[183]. Therefore, under this Act, a judgment which is obtained in a superior court of any foreign country and satisfies the requirements of Section 3 (1) of the Act shall be enforced in Nigeria, according to Reciprocal Enforcement of Judgment Act 2004. This act also provides for registration of judgment of superior courts of foreign countries, which gives reciprocal treatment to judgments of Nigeria High Courts and to which the provision of the Act has been extended.

---

[183]Cap. F35 LFN 2004

Section 9 (2) Administration Act 1920 specifies certain limits on the judgment to be registered which provides that no judgment could be registered if:-

> ➤ The original court acted without jurisdiction
> ➤ The judgment was obtained by fraud
> ➤ The judgment was in respect of a course of action, which for reasons of public policy or some other similar rule could not have been accepted by the registering court etc.

4.2 Time within which to apply for registration of judgment

Under the Ordinance Section 3(1) of the UK Ordinance provides that where a judgment has been obtained in the High Court in England or Ireland, or in the Court of Session in Scotland, the judgment creditor may apply to a High Court at any time within twelve (12) months after the date of the judgment, or such longer period as may be allowed by the court, to have the judgment registered. Based on this provision, Nigerian courts have, in a long line of cases, held that any application for registration in Nigeria of a judgment obtained in a High Court in England must be registered within a period of twelve months from the date the judgment was made otherwise such an application would be held to be time barred and refused. Although this provision suggests that the court could extend the time within which a judgment creditor may apply to register a judgment, we are not aware of any case where the court actually exercised that jurisdiction. Under Nigerian law, an application for extension of time within which to register a judgment outside the period statutorily provided would involve the exercise of the judge's discretionary power which is required to be exercised judicially and judiciously and having regard to the entire circumstances of/ the matter.

4.3 Ordinance Applicable to Money Judgment

Only a judgment to which the Ordinance applies is any judgment or order given or made by a court in any civil proceedings, whether before or after the commencement of the Ordinance, whereby any sum of money is made payable, and includes an award in proceedings or in an arbitration if the award has, in pursuance of the law in force in the place where it was made, become enforceable in the same manner as a judgment given by the court in that place. In order for an arbitral award to be elevated to the status of a judgment which can be registered and enforced under the Ordinance, the award debtor is required to have applied and obtained leave of the court in the country where the award was made to enforce the award in the same manner as a judgment of that court.

4.4 Grounds for Refusing Registration of Judgment under the Ordinance

Section 3(2) of the Ordinance provides that no judgment shall be ordered to be registered if any of the following grounds exists:

(a) the original court acted without jurisdiction

(b) the judgment debtor, being a person who was neither carrying on business nor ordinarily resident within the jurisdiction of the original court, did not voluntarily appear or otherwise submit or agree to submit to the jurisdiction of that court

(c) the judgment debtor, being the defendant in the proceedings, was not duly served with the process of the original court, and did not appear, notwithstanding that he was ordinarily resident or was carrying on business within the jurisdiction of that court or agreed to submit to the jurisdiction of that court

(d) the judgment was obtained by fraud

(e) the judgment debtor satisfies the registering court either that an appeal is pending, or that he is entitled and intends to appeal against the judgment

(f) the judgment was in respect of a cause of action which for reasons of public policy or for some other similar reason could not have been entertained by the registering court.

The unfortunate consequence of the provision of section 3(2)(b) is that if the defendant is not ordinarily resident or carrying on business within the jurisdiction of the original court and did not previously agree to submit to the jurisdiction of the foreign court, he could simply ignore the proceedings against him even if duly served with the court documents and any judgment entered against him would be unenforceable on the ground that he did not submit to the jurisdiction of the court. This was the scenario in the case of Grosvenor Casinos Ltd v. Ghassan Haloui[184] where the judgment debtor, who was not ordinarily resident in the United Kingdom, was duly served with all the court processes in Nigeria but he simply ignored them and never submitted to the jurisdiction of the English court. He successfully set aside the registration of the judgment against him based on this provision. However, the Supreme Court criticized the provision and called for its amendment. The Court held that "it is particularly alarming that when in a case like this, a person ordinarily resident in Nigeria obtains credit in England and in satisfaction issues a cheque which is later dishonoured, the judgment obtained against him cannot be enforced in Nigeria. Under section 3(2)(b) above, the judgment of a court in England cannot be enforced in Nigeria on the ground that a defendant has not submitted to the jurisdiction of the English Court. There is an urgent need to reform our law on the matter. It is an open invitation to fraud and improper conduct."

4.5 Enforcement of Foreign Judgment under the Act

Section 3(1) of the Act provides as follows:

"(1) the Minister of Justice, if he is satisfied that, in the event of the benefits conferred by this Part of this Act being extended to judgments given in the superior courts of any foreign country, substantial reciprocity of treatment will be assured as respects the enforcement in that foreign country of judgments

---

[184] (2009) LPELR – 1340 (SC)

given in the superior courts in Nigeria may by order direct- (a) that this Part of this Act shall extend to that foreign country; and (b) that such courts of that foreign country as are specified in the order shall be deemed superior courts of that country for the purposes of this Part of this Act.

4.6 Time for Registration of judgment under the Act

Section 4(1) of the Act provides that "a person being a judgment creditor under a judgment to which this Part of this Act applies, may apply to a superior court in Nigeria at any time within six years after the date of the judgment, or, where there have been proceedings by way of appeal against the judgment, after the date of the last judgment given in those proceedings, to have the judgment registered in such court, and on any such application the court shall, subject to proof of the prescribed matters and to the provisions of this Act, order the judgment to be registered." There is no evidence that the Minister of Justice has exercised his powers under section 3 of the Act to extend Part 1 of the Act to any country and, consequently, the provision of section 4 of the Act remains inchoate.

However, section 10(a) of the Act provides: "Notwithstanding any other provision of this Act:

(a) A Judgment given before the commencement of an order under section 3 of this Act applying Part I of this Act to the foreign country where the judgment was given may be registered <u>within twelve months</u> from the date of the judgment or such longer period as may be allowed by a superior court in Nigeria; and (b) Any judgment registered under the Reciprocal Enforcement of Judgments Ordinance at the time of the coming into operation of an order made under section 3 of this Act in respect of the foreign country where judgment was given shall be treated as if registered under this Act and compliance of rules applicable to the former Act shall satisfy the requirement of rules made under this Act".

In the case of Macaulay v. R. Z. B Austria[185], where the issue was the time within which to register an English judgment, the Supreme Court held that the applicable law was the Ordinance and that the judgment ought to have been registered within a period of twelve months. The court, however, considered the effect of section 10(a) of the Act and held that "…since the Minister of Justice had not yet exercised his power under section 3 of the [Act] extending the application of Part 1 of the Act to the United Kingdom where the judgment in question was given, then section 10(a) of the said Act can also apply." The Court further held as follows:

"By this provision, irrespective, regardless or in spite of any other provision in the 1990 Act, any judgment of a foreign country including United Kingdom to which Part I of that Act was not extended, can only be

---

[185] SC 109/2002. [2005] 10(12 December 2003)

registered within 12 months from the date of the judgment or any longer period allowed by the court registering the judgment since the provisions of Part I of the said Act had not been extended to it. Section 4 of the 1990 Act which speaks of registering a judgment within 6 years after the date of judgment only applies to the countries where Part I of the said Act was extended, that is to say, when the Minister made an order under the 1990 Act; and in this case it was not"

4.7 Recovering the judgment sum in Foreign Currency

Section 4(3) of the Act provides, where the sum payable under a judgment is expressed in a currency other than the currency of Nigeria, the judgment shall be registered as if it were a judgment for such sum in the currency of Nigeria as, on the basis of the rate of exchange prevailing at the date of the judgment of the original court, is equivalent to the sum payable. It is to be noted, however, that section 4(3) is under Part 1 of the Act which requires the Minister's order to come into effect and since the Minister has yet to issue an order extending Part 1 of the Act to any country section 4(3) also remains inchoate. What this means, therefore, is that until the Minister makes an order under section 3 of the Act, any judgment registered under section 10(a) of the Act can be recovered in the currency of the judgment.

CONCLUSIONS AND RECOMMENDATIONS

i.   The Constitution of the Federal Republic of Nigeria is unambiguous as to which court can handle debt issues. This is due to the importance of debt recovery in the economic contribution of companies.

ii. This area of law requires specialized training of lawyers, particularly insolvency lawyers, staff of regulatory agency.

iii. It is salutary that the constitution has wisely put debt recovery matters on High Courts as lower courts would not have the requisite background and expertise in economic, evidence and finance required to distill and adjudicate on debt recovery matters.

REFERENCES

(2019) LPELR-47309 (CA). See BANK OF IRELAND v UBN & ANOR
(1998) LPELR - 744(SC)
Standard Securities Ltd. v. Hubbard (1967) Ch. 1056 at 1059
Chatsworth Investment Ltd. v. Amoco (U.K.) Ltd. (
1968) Ch. 665, C.A. (iii)
(1982) 12 S.C.1; Green v. Green (1987) 3 NWLR (Pt.61) 480; Odu'a Investment
Co. Ltd. v. Talabi (1991) 1 NWLR (Pt.170) 761 and Governor of Oyo State v.
Folayan (1995) 8 NWLR (Pt. 413) 292. (iv)

Bullen and Leake and Jacob's Precedents of Pleadings, Twelfth Edition by I.H.
Jacobs at page 1365." per ONU, J.S.C (PP. 23-25, PARAS. A-C).
MERILL GURANTY SAVINGS & LOANS LTD v WORLD (Supra)
Per **OBASEKI-ADEJUMO, JCA** *(Pp. 15-19, paras. B-C)*
(2019) LPELR-47327

Opia V. Independent National Electoral Commission & Anor (2014) LPELR-
22185 (SC); Odutola V. University of Ilorin 18 NWLR (Pt 1156) 563 et 462.
(1998) LPELR-744 (SC) page 16, paragraphs B-C. *Per* **YAKUBU, JCA** *(Pp.
40-41, paras. E-F)*

Cap. F35 LFN 2004

(2009) LPELR – 1340 (SC)

SC 109/2002. [2005] 10(12 December 2003)

LONGITUDINAL RESEARCH INTO THE HISTORY OF DEBTS

BACKGROUND

Man, which includes companies, has tried to provide sufficiency and surplus through the request for loans. However, economic and political structures have hampered the realization of the initiatives towards borrowing. This paper has sought to examine the macro and definition of terms in order to make recommendations for more egalitarian societies.

INTRODUCTION:

Whethet Marxixt, socialist or capitalist, commerce was eponymous to debt. The necessity to collect debts existed long before currency was invented. The bartering of goods or services in return for other goods or services often led to the creation of debt as one of the parties failed sometimes to deliver their goods or services, as agreed.

A longitudinal research shows that the earliest recording of how debt was dealt with goes back to 3000BC during the ancient civilization of Sumer who populated an area that is now modern-day South East Iraq. The book of Chronicles narrated how a debtor who was unable to pay a debt along with their family and servants became debt slaves. They were forced to work for the creditor until such time that their physical labour had repaid the debt. In some cases, it took years to repay the debt, which could even be passed on to the following generation of the debtor's family. Debt slaves became common throughout many ancient civilizations. However, some of the more liberal early societies introduced forms of debt forgiveness or allowed debts to be discharged after a specific period of time. However, Abrahamic religions, discouraged lending and creditors were prohibited from seeking to collect debts.

Before the medieval times, and post Adam Smith, John Maynard Keynes, Milton Friedman etc, businesses and national economies needed finance for expansion, growth, development, or business rescue. The Marshal Plan was an example of continental initiative for European bail out. In the modern times, statistics show that as at 2017, about 2.3 million Nigerians owe banks ₦15.9 trillions. The Asset Management Corporation of Nigeria (AMCON) has expressed that only three hundred and fifty (350) debtors in Nigeria owe it the humongous amount of N3.6 trillion (three trillion, six billion naira). With low productivity, large scale corruption, low savings, and high consumption patterns, Nigerian institutions have had to borrow from local and external sources to bridge gaps in funding, control the national economy and secure maximum welfare, freedom and happiness of citizens on the basis of social justice, equality of status and opportunity.

The Marshall Plan assisted the development of Europe, and regional initiatives like the ADB, NDIC, AMCON have emerged in the loan recovery space. The celebrated case of Salomon v Salomon & Brothers od 1894 came to the fore. Mr. Salomon had transferred his business of boot making, initially run as a sole proprietorship, to a company (Salomon Ltd.), incorporated with members comprising himself and his family. The price for such transfer was paid to Salomon by way of shares, and debentures having a floating charge (security against debt) on the assets of the company. Later, when the company's business went into liquidation, Salomon's right of recovery (secured through floating charge) against the debentures superceded the claims of unsecured creditors, who would, thus, have recovered nothing from the liquidation proceeds.

To avoid an alleged unjust exclusion, the liquidator, on behalf of the unsecured creditors, alleged that the company was a sham, being essentially an agent of Salomon. Since Salomon was the principal, he was personally liable for its debt. In other words, the liquidator sought to overlook the separate personality of Salomon Ltd., distinct from its member Mr. Salomon so as to make Salomon personally liable for the company's debt as if he continued to conduct the business as a sole trader.

For corporations, there are various reasons for debt defaults e.g. like mismanagement, micro-economic headwinds, environmental and political risks, many debtors default in making payments at the agreed time frame or/and debtor(s) blatant refusal to pay preferring to dishonor agreements.

In Nigeria, particularly, the Nigerian state suffers from Quotidian reality "group grievance," "economic decline," "human capital flight," "demographic pressure," "weak and corrupt public service," "deterioration in the rule of law," deterioration in human rights," and "ineffective security apparatus." It may be no exaggeration to add even that "state legitimacy is in doubt." A descent to self-help in debt recovery can translate to a recipe for chaos, which must be prevented by a process of Law.

There are so many reasons why some debtors do not pay their debts as at when due. Some of the reasons include divergence between theory and praxis.

1. The debtor's mismanagement of the loan sum
2. The diversion of the loan sum into unprofitable ventures, even for marrying more wives and for political participation.

3. The debtor may suffer actual inability to pay due to failure of the venture or project for which he borrowed the money. In the Mikibanga's case,[186] the plaintiff debtor obtained an agricultural loan from the defendant creditor bank and mortgaged his house to the bank as security for the loan. He used the loan sum to enhance his poultry farm which indeed was the agreed purpose of the loan. Later, however a mishap set in through no fault of his and he suffered severe loss of the fowls. His poultry business nose dived sharply and as a result, he found himself unable to pay the loan sum.

4. Loans obtained for the purpose of executing government contracts. When this happens, most contractors and business men rely on government patronage and they frequently borrow from banks, institutions and individuals to execute the government contracts. Very often the contractor/debtor may have performed the contract for which he had borrowed money, Government fail to pay him for the contract, eventually he too will become unable to repay the loan sum to the creditor. An illustrative case of the role of government in non-payment by debtors is Nyoyoko v Akwa Ibom State Government & 2ors.[187] The plaintiff had borrowed money from a bank for the purpose of purchasing some typewriters for supply to the then Akwa Ibom State House of Assembly in 1992. After he had supplied the items but before he could be paid, the military took over government and dissolved all civil democratic structures including the State House of Assembly. Even though all the supply / contractual documents were available to the new military government it still did not pay the plaintiff until the plaintiff went to court which ordered payment.

5. Negligence on the part of the debtor or deliberate refusal to pay.

6. Debt.loans as low hanging fruits

1.3 DEFINITION OF TERMS:

i. Debt:

Debt in the context of this article is a fixed or certain obligation to pay money or some valuable thing or things; either in the present or in the future. In *Eco Bank Plc V Hon Lukpata John Udo*[188] a "debt" was defined as a specific sum of money due by agreement or otherwise." "The action of debt lies where a party claims the recovery of a debt; that is, a liquidated or certain sum of money due him. [189] The action is based upon contract, but the contract may be implied, in fact or in law, as well as expressed and it may be either a simple contract or a

---

[186] Mikibanga & Sons (Nig) & anor. V. African Continental Bank PLC.
[187] (2020) LPELR-49691 (CA)
[188] *2012 LPELR-13926 CA*
[189] See Black's Law Dictionary, 8th edition p.432 where the learned authors referred to Benjamin J. Shipman Handbook of common-Law Pleading edited by Henry Winthrop Ballantine, 3rd edition 1923 paragraph 52 page 132 where the learned author wrote that:

specialty. The most common instances of its use are for debts: (a) upon unilateral contracts expressed or implied in fact (b) upon quasi-contractual obligations having the force and effect of simple contracts (c) upon bonds and covenants under seal (d) upon judgment, or obligations of record (e) upon obligations imposed by statute."[190]

In summary, a debt exists where a certain amount of money is owed from one person (the creditor) to another (the debtor) due to certain agreements. Contracts are entered and executed between parties for various reasons and when there is a breach or failure of party to perform his part of the contract, and a debt arises, the aggrieved party or in this case, the creditor may commence a process to recover the said debt.

The meaning of debt was further defined in the case of *Nigerian Postal Services V Insight Engineering Company Ltd.*[191] *Viz;*

"What then is a debt? I think a useful guide may be found in Jowitt's Dictionary of English Law where the following definition and explanation as to the nature of the "debt" were given. A debt is "... a sum of money due from one person to another. An action of debt lay where a person claimed the recovery of a liquidated or certain sum of money affirmed to be due to him; it was generally founded on some contract alleged to have taken place between the parties, or on some matter of fact from which the law would imply a contract between them. There is aspecies mentioned in the books, called debt in the detinet, which lay for the specific recovery of goods, under a contract to deliver them.... A debt exists when a certain sum of money is owing from one person (the debtor) to another (the creditor). Hence 'debt' is properly opposed to unliquidated damages...; to liability, when used in the sense of an inchoate or contingent debt; and to certain obligations not enforceable by ordinary process ... 'Debt' denotes not only the obligation of the debtor to pay, but also the right of the creditor to receive and enforce payment. Debts are of various kinds, according to their origin ... Debts may be created under the provisions of various statutes.."[192]

ii. A DEBTOR:

A debtor is **a company or an individual who owes money**. If the debt is in the form of a loan from a financial institution, the debtor is referred to as a borrower, and if the debt is in the form of securities such as bonds the debtor is referred to as an issuer. A person who is in debt or under financial obligation to another is also referred to as a Debtor.

---

[190] *Per* **TUR, JCA** *(Pp. 13-14, paras. B-A)*
[191] *2006 LPELR - 8240 (CA)*
[192] *Per* **IKONGBEH, JCA** *(Pp. 22-23, paras. C-D)*

iii. A CREDITOR:

A creditor or lender is a party that has a claim to the services of a second party. It is a person or institution to whom money is owed. The first party, in general, has provided some property or service to the second party under the assumption that the second party will return an equivalent property and service. A creditor is also an entity (person or institution) that extends credit by giving another entity permission to borrow money intended to be repaid in the future. A business that provides supplies or services to a company or individual and does not demand payment immediately is also considered a creditor, based on the fact that the client owes the business money for services already rendered.

v. Debt Recovery:

Debt Recovery is the process of
making people or companies pay the money which they owe to
other people or companies when they have not paid back the debt at
the time that was agreed.

It is also the process of recovering a debt from a debtor(s). This arises when the due date for payment of the debt has elapsed but the debtor has refused to make such payment even when demands for such payment of the loan had been made.

In Nigeria, the limitation period for debt recovery that arises from a simple contract is six (6) years excluding the year the contract was entered into and executed. The court has the power to hear and determine an action for debt recovery and enforce payment on the debtor. The law has provided for a lawful process and procedure for debt recovery. It must be pointed out that owing debt is a civil wrong, and not a criminal wrong. Thus, the Police and other security agencies have no power under the law to arrest, prosecute or to take any action against a person for failure to pay debts.

In the case of McLaren & Ors v Jennings[193], the Appeal Court ruled that debt collection is not part of the duties to the police.[194] The defendants supplied the vehicle used by the police to go to Kano to demand and recover a debt and not for the purpose of investigating an offence. The arrest, in the circumstance, was wrongful. Justice Ayo Salami[195] said in the lead judgment, thus, "In short, the appellants and the policemen they took to Kano were there to collect debt which is not one of the several duties assigned to the police under the provisions of the Police Act to which the court was directed and the court has not been able to find another provision of the Act empowering or constituting the Nigerian Police Force to be one of a debt or rent collector."

The Apex court ruled that issues involving breach of contract are not part of the primary duties of the police, while wondering how the police could "easily

---

[193]

[194] McLaren & Ors V Jennings (2002)
[195]

metamorphose" a civil matter to a criminal case.[196] Likewise, the Apex court dismissed the conviction of the appellant, who had breached a contract agreement to deliver calf giraffes to the Rivers State Ministry of Culture and Tourism through one Sokari Davies.

Many cases confirm that a cause of action is deemed to accrue when the debtor refuses to pay after a demand is made.[197]

See also Victor v. UBA Plc[198] and Okonta v. Egbuna[199] were referred to for the position.[200]

Progressively the law has sought to ensure free flow of loans for expansion and to ensure economic stability. However, the law ensures provision of capital is not jeopardized in the recovery of their loans so that they can go round to those who require them for socio-economic purposes.

CONCLUSIONS AND RECOMMENDATIONS

The origin of dents shows a cultural transformation rom pure agricultural produce, seedlings, money, batter and journey.

The variants has been increasing since the industrial and digital revolutions.

The subjects of loans and debts remain the same except that institutions and financial structures that give and regulate debts and recoveries vary from country to country.

For all these categories of participants in loan recovery process, training is needed even for the judges, receivers, liquidators and the debtors.

---

[196] Kure v C.O.P (2020)
[197] Union Bank of Nigeria Ltd Vs Oki (1999) 8 NWLR (Pt 614) 255, Amede Vs United Bank for Africa Plc (2003) 8 NWLR (Pt.1090) 623." Per **ABIRU, JCA** *(P. 36, paras. D-E).*
[198] (2007) LPELR-90413 (CA) Supra
[199] (2013) LPELR-21253 (CA) Supra
[200] Maersk Nig. Ltd. v. Uma Invest. Co. Ltd. (2013) LPELR-21247 (CA), Onokomma v. Union Bank of Nigeria, Plc (2017) LPELR-42748 (CA); Omosowan v. Chiedozie (1998) 9 NWLR (Pt. 566) 477." *Per* **GARBA, JCA** *(Pp. 17-22, paras. E-A)*

PARTIES TO DEBT RECOVERY PROCESS

1. BACKGROUND

The main thrust of this paper is to elucidate the proper persons empowered to collect debts in Nigeria. A comparative approach of what obtains in the USA has also been shown in this study. With the developments in trade and finance, the institutions involved in debt recovery process have increased from primary financing institutions to third party securities traders, swaps and derivatives participants and regulatory agencies like Assets Management Company of Nigeria, Nigerian Deposit Insurance Corporation, EFCC etc. This paper attempts to elucidate the parties involved in debt collection. No attempt has been made to analyze informal debt collection strategies of local communities like the youth bodies levying execution on debtors assets.

The process of debt collection in many cases involves a debt collector or a debt collection agency, whose primary object is to ensure that debts owed to creditors are successfully recovered. In order to successfully recover these debts, the debt collector has to conduct the necessary search on all the necessary details of the debtor. Not only should the debt collector conduct search on the debtor, there is also need for a proper examination of the debt in question to better understand what advice maybe best suited for the case and most beneficial to the creditor. The debt collector could suggest a waiver, debt restructuring, debt adjusting, debt adjustment or even a debt write-off.

> The US Supreme Court ruled that a consumer claimant under the Federal Fair Debt Collection Practices Act ("FDCPA") has one year from the alleged violation to file a suit.[201] The one-year statute of limitation begins at the time of the alleged wrongful act, even if the consumer is unaware of the purported violation. The court did, however leave the door open for a consu mer to bring suit beyond one year if the debt collector fraudulently conceals its actions. The court rejected an expansion of the period of time by which a victim of unlawful debt collection must file suit. Section 1692k(d) thereof states that a lawsuit "may be brought . . . within one year from the date on which the violation occurs." The debtor argued that the court should interpret the statute to give a victim one year from the time that he or she learned of the wrongful act to commence litigation. Since Congress enacted statutory limitation periods that begin to run at the time

---

[201] *In Rotkiske v. Klemm*, 589 U.S. (2019) ,

of the wrongful act's discovery but failed to include such language in the Fair Debt Collection Practices Act, the court refused to create an exception that congress itself elected not to include.

On May 15, 2017, the United States Supreme Court in *Midland Funding, LLC v. Johnson*, held that a debt collector who files a bankruptcy proof of claim on a time-barred debt does not violate the FDCPA.[202]

The dispute in *Midland* arose after debt collector Midland Funding, LLC (*"Midland"*) filed a proof of claim in a debtor's Chapter 13 proceeding. The debt upon which Midland based its claim was outside the applicable state statute of limitations. Following an objection by Johnson, the bankruptcy court denied Midland's claim, and the debtor later brought suit for an FDCPA violation.

The District Court dismissed the debtor's case after holding that the FDCPA did not apply in bankruptcy. However, the U.S. Court of Appeals for the 11th Circuit later reversed the decision and determined that Midland's conduct in filing the proof of claim on clearly time-barred debt was in fact an FDCPA violation.[203]

The Supreme Court found that Midland's conduct was neither unfair nor deceptive under the FDCPA. Specifically, the Court explained that pursuant to the plain language of the Bankruptcy Code, a proof of claim does not have to be enforceable at the time of its filing. Thus, the court reasoned that, filing a proof of claim on a time-barred debt was contemplated by the Bankruptcy Code, and would therefore not be considered deceptive. The filing a proof of claim on a time-barred debt did not rise to the level of unfair or unconscionable conduct prohibited under the FDCPA. Relying on holdings from a number of federal appellate courts that previously determined that filing a collection lawsuit on time-barred debt violated the FDCPA, the debtor argued that the filing of a proof of claim is the equivalent of filing a collection lawsuit, and as such should be considered a violation. The Court disagreed, and pointed to the following key factors which distinguish a collection action from filing a proof of claim in a bankruptcy: (1) the customer initiates the bankruptcy and would therefore not be at risk of paying a time-barred debt to avoid a collection lawsuit; (2) the trustee's supervision and the procedural rules in place in a bankruptcy would prevent a bankruptcy estate from paying out on time-barred or otherwise unenforceable claims; and (3) there is the possibility that the filing of the claim will actually benefit the debtor because the debt would be discharged if the debtor is able to successfully complete his/her bankruptcy plan.

---

[202] No. 16-348, 2017 WL 2039159 (U.S. May 15, 2017),
[203] *See Johnson v. Midland Funding, LLC,* 823 F.3d 1334 (11th Cir. 2016), *cert. granted,* 137 S. Ct. 326, 196 L. Ed. 2d 212 (2016).

The Supreme Court's holding in *Midland* reaffirms the Seventh Circuit's position in *Owens v. LVNV Funding, LLC*, 832 F.3d 726 (7th Cir., 2016), whereby the Seventh Circuit Court of Appeals held that a "claim" under the Bankruptcy Code encompassed more than legally enforceable obligations under the relevant state law, and therefore the act of filing a proof of claim on stale debt was not an automatic FDCPA violation.

2. TYPES OF DEBT COLLECTORS

The types of debt collection agencies include:

a. First-party Agencies: These are usually subsidiaries or departments of the company that owns the debt; or the creditor. They are called first party because they are a part of the original contract.

b. Third-party Agencies: A third-party agency is usually not a party to the original contract. The creditor assigns accounts directly to such an agency on a contingency-fee basis. The collection or third party agency makes money only if money is collected from the debtor (often known as a "No Collection - No Fee" basis).

c. Debt Buyers: The debt buyer purchases accounts and debts from creditors for a percentage of the value of the debt and may subsequently pursue the debtor for the full balance due, including any interest that accrues under the terms of the original loan or credit agreement. This is most times the case when Asset Management Corporation of Nigeria (AMCON) is involved in a debt recovery situation. The agency purchases debts from banks or financial houses at a particular percentage which may have reduced the value of the debts, but bears some risks involved in the recovery of the debt.

d. A debt collector must be careful not to employ any of the following means or methods for debt recovery: harassment, abuse or oppression of the debtor, use of threat or violence, use of obscene languages, employ the use of thugs, mystical, occultism or any diabolical methods; and most of all, the use of the police or other security agents to arrest a debtor. The Police are not empowered by any statutes to recover debts as they are not debt collectors. The court expressly mentioned that;

"it has been stated many times that the police have no business in enforcement of debt settlements or recovering of civil debts for banks or anybody".[204]

In *Henson v. Santander Consumer, USA, Inc.*,[205] Santander purchased the plaintiffs' defaulted debt from the loan originator after acting as the loan servicer. After Santander began its collection efforts, Henson and the accompanying class of plaintiffs brought suit, claiming that Santander's debt collection practices violated the FDCPA. Santander moved to dismiss the claim

---

[204] Oceanic Securities Int. Ltd V. Balogun & Ors (2012) LPELR-9218
[205] 817 F.3d 131, 136 (4th Cir. 2016), *cert. granted*, 137 S. Ct. 810, 196 L. Ed. 2d 595 (2017)

on the basis that it was exempted from the FDCPA because it was not acting as a third party debt collector, but was instead seeking repayment on its own debt. The District Court agreed with Santander, with the Fourth Circuit Court of Appeals also affirming the District Court's decision. Henson appealed to the United States Supreme Court".

The Supreme Court's review comes in the face of a circuit split on this issue, with the Fourth, Ninth and Eleventh circuits holding that collectors of debt purchased after default are not debt collectors subject to the FDCPA, while the Third, Fifth, Sixth and Seventh circuits, and the District of Columbia Court of Appeals have taken the contrary position.

Not surprisingly, April's oral arguments focused primarily on the definition of "debt collector" under the FDCPA. The Act defines a "debt collector" as "any person...who regularly collects...debts owed or due...another." Henson took the position that debts were "owed" to the originator of the loan, but "due" to the debt buyer. Thus, under such reasoning, a debt purchaser could be considered a "debt collector" under the FDCPA because it was collecting on a debt "owed" to the originator of the loan (notwithstanding the fact that it was also collecting on a loan now "due" to the debt purchaser).

Conversely, Santander took the position that as the current holder of the debt, it was merely collecting on its own debt (the same as any creditor would) and was therefore not subject to the purview of the FDCPA.

With little guidance from past precedents as to the definition of "debt collector" under the Act, both sides also argued steadfastly for consideration of the policy implications or their respective positions. Henson and the consumer plaintiffs argued that debt collectors could circumvent the requirements of the FDCPA by simply purchasing debt they intended to collect on. Conversely, Santander argued that a purchaser of debt has very different motives than that of a debt collector, and it was for this reason that debt purchasers were intentionally excluded from the FDCPA.

e. Liquidators

A liquidator is a person appointed by the court to wind up the affairs of a company and distribute the assets among creditors and contributories in accordance with the law and the articles of the company.

Under S. ... CAMA, Liquidators have extensive powers and duties to investigate a company's affairs and in some cases to pursue its directors. However, the primary duty of the liquidator is to increase the assets of the company, collect in all the assets and realise it at the best possible price to maximize the funds available for distribution to the creditors.

In Johnson v Odeku[206], the defendant's account ceased to be in credit in 1958 and he made his last withdrawal in 1960. The bank then went into liquidation and in 1966, the liquidator instituted proceedings on the bank's behalf against the defendant to recover the amount of the overdraft plus interest.

It must be pointed out that when a registered company goes into liquidation, it is no longer run by its owners and the liquidator must work out who the business owes money to, and pays them back using any assets or money left in the business. Those owed money are called creditors.

In the case of AKAHALL & SONS LTD V NDIC[207]

"Under the Companies Winding Up Rules 1983, a debt is proved against a wound-up Company by delivering or sending through post to the liquidator an affidavit verifying the debt, which must contain or refer to the statement of account showing the particulars of the debt and whether the creditor is or is not a secured creditor. The liquidator has the power to examine and admit or reject every proof lodged with it. It is only when a creditor is dissatisfied with the decision by the liquidator that he can apply to the Court to reverse or vary the decision."[208]

In addition to resolving the current circuit court split, the Supreme Court's decision is also expected to drastically impact state collection agency and debt collection laws that mirror the FDCPA's provisions.

  f. Receivership
     A receivership is a court-appointed tool that can assist creditors to recover funds in default . Having a receivership in place makes it easier for a lender to recover funds that are owed to them if a borrower defaults on a loan.
     Generally, the receiver's role is to:
     i. collect and sell enough of the secured assets to repay the debt owed to the secured creditor (this may include selling assets or the company's business)
     ii. pay out the money collected in the order required by law

According to the provisions of S582(1) of Companies and Allied Matters, an official receiver means the Deputy Chief Registrar of the Federal High Court or an officer designated for that purpose by the Chief Judge of the Court.

In the case of Olawale Akoni SAN v ASCON Oil Company Limited[209], Rainoil Limited, the lawful owner of the property including the Petrol Station located at Block 36 Admiralty Way, Lekki, Lagos, acquired the property which was

---

[206] [1967] NCLR 361
[207] (2017) LPELR-41984
[208] Per **AKA'AHS, JSC** (Pp. 8-9, paras. E-A)
[209] FHC/L/CS/567/2020

formerly owned by ASCON Oil Company Limited from Stanbic IBTC Bank Plc, in exercise of the Bank's right of sale under a duly registered Deed of Legal Mortgage. STANBIC's Right of Sale pursuant to the Deed of Legal Mortgage was legally and duly triggered, after ASCON failed to pay their debts to the bank, and upon crystallisation, STANBIC duly appointed a Receiver Mr Olawale Akoni, SAN over the said assets of ASCON by STANBIC.

The Receiver sought and obtained a subsisting Mandatory Order of the Federal High Court dated 15/5/20.[210] via which order, the Assistant Inspector General (AIG) of Police, Zone 2 Police Command was mandated by the Court to grant Police Protection to the Receiver in the execution of his powers as duly appointed by STANBIC with respect to the said Property.

Consequently, and upon payment of the consideration sum for the purchase of the Property, STANBIC assigned and out rightly transferred all its interests, and rights over the said property to Rainoil Limited, by virtue of which Rainoil became the lawful and rightful owners of the Property, including Petrol Station. As new owners of the Property, Rainoil were put in vacant and peaceable possession by the Receiver on 20/5/20.

ASCON, being dissatisfied with the actions of the Receiver with the take over and sale of the said property, filed a motion at the Federal High Court to challenge the acts of the Receiver and bank's right to sell the said property to Rainoil, and to set aside the Mandatory Order of the Federal High Court.

On the 24/7/20, Justice Liman of the Federal High Court gave his ruling and validated the actions of the Receiver. He further posited that the prayer of ASCON to set aside, reverse, nullify and or suspend the steps taken pursuant to the actions and powers of the Receiver in the sale of the said property to Rainoil, can only be reversed or considered upon the institution of a substantive suit. Suffice it to say that ASCON who are affiliated with Quest Oil, having failed in challenging the Ruling of the Federal High Court, have resorted to fraudulent and illegal means to deprive Rainoil of their legitimate proprietary rights, by making attempts to forcefully take over the property through fictitious and malicious means, notably on 4/8/20, 16/12/20 and more recently, on 13/8/21, when some unidentified Officers of ASCON and QUEST accompanied by 20 armed Mobile Policemen from the office of AIG, Zone 2, Onikan, in the company of hoodlums invaded the above mentioned property once again, under the guise of executing the same Ruling of the Federal High Court dated 24/7/20 per Liman J in the said case, which they have already appealed against. They unleashed acts of brigandage and malicious disruption of Rainoil's business operations, including forcefully removing Staff dispensing petrol from the Forecourt, damaging property, the canopy, pylon signages, and illegally and

---

[210] Suit No. FHC/L/CS/567/2020 Olawale Akoni SAN v ASCON Oil Company Limited,

forcefully seizing two Trucks loaded with 90,000 litres of petrol, belonging to Rainoil which was and parked within the premises.

Preceding the above, the office of the Commissioner of Police Lagos State and AIG of Police Zone 2 Onikan, had written to the Deputy Chief Registrar of the Federal High Court, Ikoyi, Lagos on three occasions, requesting the court to confirm the order granted by Justice Liman in the said Suit No. FHC/L/CS/567/2020 – Olawale Akoni (SAN) v Ascon Oil Company Limited and permission to execute. The Deputy Chief Registrar in reply to their letters dated 4/8/21 and 9/8/21 respectively, replied to the request of the AIG, Zone 2, Onikan, and confirmed that the said Ruling of Justice Liman in the suit is valid and subsisting until it is set aside by the court; and that there were pending motions and a Notice of Appeal filed in respect of the aforementioned suit by ASCON; and the fact that the Court Order had been executed, further established that Sheriff's office could enforce/ execute the said order twice.

Accordingly, it came as a shock to learn that the Police disregarded all responses of the Deputy Chief Registrar /Admiralty Marshal Sub, and opted to act in contempt of the court. More appalling is that there was no substantive court order or legal justification for the actions of ASCON and Policemen from the office of the AIG, Zone 2, Onikan, including the forceful entry and unlawful repossession of Rainoil's property. The Federal High Court has since disassociated itself from this illegal act of brigandage and lawlessness, exhibited by the Police and Officers of ASCON and QUEST.

The Company Administrators

A company administrator is one of the agents that can assist in the recovery of debt. The Company Administrator for an organization can manage organization profile information, manage the roster, view and update account information for organization members, and register members for events, and manage billing for the organization. Section 505 of the CAMA gives the company administrator the power to manage the affairs of the company.

The administrator's main role is to promote the recovery of the company, it may be that he feels it is more suitable to come to arrangement with the company's creditors, sell the business as a going concern or realize assets to pay the company's creditors.

3. Recommendations & Conclusions

i.   Due process and Rule of Law require that debtors and creditors be given fair attention and recognition in the loan recovery process.

ii.   The various debt collectors have their various legal obligations, powers and rights as provided by the Law, some of which are to protect assets against dissipation and diminution. The due process of the law must always be followed.

iii.   The more the debts, the more the complexity and amount of debts to GDPs which require longitudinal regulation and legal surveillance to ensure economic well being. The law should ensure that funds are maintained as common wealth for utilization by all for economic development.

Pertinent and Pragmatic Dimensions of ADR in AMCON's Debt Recovery Process

Abstract

*In 2010, the Asset Management Corporation of Nigeria (**AMCON**) was set up with the aim of recovering the huge debts owed by obligors. In spite of efforts made by the organisation and enhanced AMCON recovery powers the amount of Non-Performing Loans (NPLs) recovered has remained staggering at about ₦5 trillion. Since AMCON's NPLs are largely collateralized, the Corporation exercises powers and rights over the assets in its position as a secured creditor. However, where the NPL forming the Eligible Bank Assets is not collateralised, the remedial power of AMCON has been the right to pursue the debtor to recover the loans as an unsecured creditor.*

Conceptually, the mandate of AMCON is not strictly about winding-up companies but to midwife corporate rescues within the legal frame work that assures recovery of debts granted for business. Thus, AMCON safeguards creditors' securities and purchase toxic and bad loans from commercial banks and remove them from the balance sheet of the banks. In the process, AMCON has returned some banks to liquidity so as to preserve and protect depositors' funds through aggressive pursuit of the recovery of debts purchased. Where the remedies of sale and foreclosure, are readily available, reference to ADR has been a good option as concessions and compromises have been made ADRs. Also, resolving complexities in loan syndication take time and the multiplicity of parties create diverse problems in the ADR process which pose new challenges when each of the parties is insistent on rights created in the loan documentation.

1. Introduction

The overall purview of the AMCON Act[211] is not necessarily based on the precepts of insolvency and bankruptcy laws but that the creditors of financially unhealthy companies do not suffer unnecessary dissipation of their investments in companies, which jeopardises the finance industry.

To buttress AMCON's efforts, the amended AMCON Act of 2015 grants AMCON additional responsibility to take all legally reasonable action to

---

*Dr Kathleen Okafor, FCIArb. (Assoc. Prof.). Dean Baze University, Abuja.
[211] AMCON Act, No. 4, 2010

"recover" funds of ailing companies and restore companies to financial viability, if possible. Thus, Receivers/Managers appointed by AMCON are to "cause to be prepared a detailed and comprehensive plan for the rehabilitation of the debtor-company or debtor-entity".

To this regard, section 48 of the AMCON Act empowers AMCON, as a body corporate, to either act as, or appoint a receiver for a debtor company whose assets have been charged, mortgaged or pledged as security to AMCON and can also appoint a third party entity to act as a receiver on its behalf. This is a unique departure from the provision of S. 387(1) (c) of the Companies and Allied Matters Act (CAMA) which among others, disqualifies appointment of corporate bodies.

Any receiver appointed under the AMCON Act is empowered to (i) realise the assets of the debtor company; (ii) enforce the individual liability of the shareholders and directors of the debtor company, and also (iii) manage the affairs of the debtor company.

Nevertheless, in the performance of their duties under the AMCON Act, Receivers/Managers are bound to adhere to the provisions of the relevant deed of appointment which appointed them and are in no way limited to the powers enumerated under section 48 of the AMCON Act.

Deposit money banks (DMBs) usually back up loans by registered legal charges/mortgages or other securities that make loans realisable without resort to long drawn battles in court. Other securities such as domiciliation and assignments of proceeds are also common in secured lending. In the case of registered charges/mortgages, realising the loan is relatively easy as statutory power of sale and foreclosures are available remedies usually provided in the security documents (without reference to court)[212].

In 2019, additional powers enacted under the AMCON (Amendment Act) 2019 which empowers the agency to by-pass any legal or procedural restrictions, specifically to enable the Agency gain access to any computer system, place any bank account of a debtor under surveillances well as obtain access to any computer system component, electronic or mechanical device of any debtor to locate funds belonging to any debtor.

2. Legal Remedies Open to Creditors

Inevitably, debtors and their counsels formulate all possible defences to delay payment of their debts, not necessarily due to fraud but because of macro-economic constraints. The ambit of remedies available to creditors was elucidated by the Supreme Court which has also reinforced the power of Banks to sell and realise loans in appropriate circumstances[213]. In that case, a dispute

---

[212]UBN Plc v Olori Motors Ltd (1998) 5 NWLR (Pt. 554)-347.
[213] ACB v Ihekwoaba (2003) 16 NWLR (Pt 846) 249: Okonkwo v CCB (2003) 8 NWLR (Pt 822) 3478

involved a tenancy agreement between the parties which contained an arbitration clause to the effect that disputes were to be referred to a Sole Arbitrator to be appointed by the President of the "Chartered Institute of Arbitration (London) Nigerian Chapter". The arbitration proceeded and a final award was made[214]. The award at the High Court of Lagos State was challenged on the ground, *inter alia*, that there was no valid arbitration agreement between the parties. The contention was that "there is no body/organisation known as THE CHARTERED INSTITUTE OF ARBITRATION (LONDON) NIGERIAN CHAPTER and as such, there cannot be a referral for arbitration to a non-existent body." The High Court dismissed the challenge. The Court of Appeal, however, disagreed and held that – "... since there is in effect no body/organisation known as the Chartered Institute of Arbitration (London) Nigerian chapter, the clause itself is unenforceable."

With the availability of remedies such as foreclosure, statutory sale and appointment of receivers/managers, a party such as AMCON usually pursues settled legal remedies where possible. This is, particularly so in cases of toxic loans whose values continue to depreciate due to delays or inaction on the part of the creditors.

In cases of syndicated loans where there are two or more lenders may be secured or unsecured, the issue of priority of settlement in the event of default or pure interpretation of the clauses usually arises.

Furthermore, some Non-Performing Loans have fraudulent or political undertones e.g. misrepresentation, political patronage, or in-house bank creditors utilising third party legal mortgage, forged title documents, (with collusion of land officers in the Registry). In the event of default, the fraud may constitute a key defence to loan enforcement when parties go to Alternative Dispute Resolution (ADR). Apart from using state security enforcement apparatus such as the Economic and Financial Crimes Commission (EFCC) or the police, parties will usually insist on prosecution in addition to civil remedies in court as opposed to Alternative Dispute Resolution (ADR).

Some credit disputes also exhibit overcharged interest rates or domiciliation without any mortgage or charge and therefore not have strong chances of being resolved by ADR. The LMDC has made giant strides in this area, particularly where it is shown that both the bank and the debtor are committed to a long term mutual beneficial interest or are still desirous of preserving the relationship they have cultivated overtime.

3. The Wide Powers of AMCON as a Receiver
a. Power to Realise the Assets of Debtor Companies

Based on the AMCON Act, AMCON can sell the entire assets of a debtor company to liquidate the debt obligations of a company in favour of its

---

[214]Starline (Nig.) Ltd & Anor v Onyeagocha & Anor (2018) CA LPELR-41268

creditors. By Section 48(3) of the AMCON Act, AMCON's powers to realise assets extends to assets not specifically charged, mortgaged or pledged as security in relation to the Eligible Bank Assets (EBA) acquired by AMCON. However, the Receiver must recognize the rights of other secured creditors and third parties.[215]

If a winding up order is made or provisional liquidator appointed, no action or proceeding shall proceed or commence except by leave of court. The true purpose of the appointment of a receiver/manager is to safeguard the Assets and properties of the company under receivership for the benefit of those entitled to it, particularly debenture holders. On assets not under receivership, the powers of directors supersede the powers of the Receiver[216] as legally a debtor company does not lose its corporate identity (nor its title to the goods) by the mere fact that a receivership process has commenced.[217]

Also, the existence of a prior encumbrance on the Eligible Bank Assets (EBA) acquired by AMCON does not inhibit the exercise of this power as AMCON has statutory powers to redeem or discharge such security over the EBA, even where a vesting order in respect of such security has been made.

b. *Power to enforce individual liability of shareholders and directors of the debtor company*

Under s.48 of the AMCON Act, the statement of affairs of the debtor company as given to the Receiver/Manager, upon his appointment as Receiver/Manager usually indicates individual liabilities of the Shareholders and Directors of such the debtor company.

Accordingly, AMCON can enforce these liabilities of directors/individual shareholders stated in the Statement of Affairs. A Receiver/Manager appointed under the AMCON Act can realise any asset or funds of the debtor company found in the possession of the directors and shareholders based on section 61 of the AMCON Act, which defines "Debtor" or "Debtor Company" to include a guarantor and director of such company.

Usually, an audit exercise of the debtor company is undertaken by the Receiver/Manager to ensure that all assets of directors and shareholders in relation to the debt are fully realized.

Notably is that the powers of the Receiver/Manager appointed, are not limited to calling up uncalled capital of the company[218] under CAMA (against the relevant

---

[215] The proviso to section 48(3) of the AMCON Act (as amended) 2015

[216] S. 417 CAMA –European Soaps & Detergent Ltd. V MW Bear & Co. Ltd. (2017) LPELR – 41863 (CA); Emodi v Emodi (2007)4 NWLR pt. (1024) 412.

[217] Utuk v The Liquidator (Utuk Construction Marketing Company Ltd.)ANOR. (2009) LPELR – 4322(CA)

[218] Eleventh Schedule (para. 19) CAMA

shareholder)[219], but extends to enforcing the personal liability of directors and officers of a company who cannot pay their debt. This provision is confined to situations where the company received loan or other property for a particular purpose, but the money or property was fraudulently diverted for other purposes.[220]

c. Power to manage the affairs of the Debtor Company

Legally, the Receiver is not bound by the AMCON Act to manage the business of the debtor company. Where he intends to manage the affairs of the company and the debtor-business is viable enough, he must submit a comprehensive rehabilitation plan to ensure that the viability of the debtor business is maximised.

Under the AMCON Act, the Receiver has inherent powers to manage the debtor company and need not be specially appointed as a manager to execute such statutory duties. This provision accords with the legal position of section 393 of CAMA where the Receiver must also be appointed Manager before he can manage the affairs of the debtor company.

By virtue of Sections 48(4) – 48(9) of the AMCON Act, the Receiver must proceed to effectively manage the affairs of the debtor company through an Election/Notice and Rehabilitation Plan.

4. Obligations of the Receiver/Manager under the AMCON Act

Judicially, a Receiver/Manager has the following distinct legal obligations[221]:

a. To manage the affairs of the Company in the name and on behalf of the debtor company for the benefit of the debtor company;
b. To be a fiduciary or trustee of the debtor company and all its Creditors (including AMCON);
c. To strictly adhere to debt priority ranking prescribed under section 494 of CAMA. The priority ranking under s.494 thereof states preferential payments as all local rates and charges due from the company payable 12 months before that date; pension contribution, wages and salaries, accrued holiday remuneration.

The term "fiduciary" under 3(b) here above, was defined by the Court of Appeal as *"A very broad term embracing both technical, fiduciary relations and those informal relations which exist wherever one man trusts in or relies upon another. One founded on trust or confidence reposed by one person in the integrity and fidelity of another..."*[222]beyond the ordinary status of debt recovery agent.

---

[8] S. 37 CAMA
[220] Section 290 CAMA
[221]Section 48(5) & (6) of the AMCON Act
[222]Per Bage JCA (P. 20 paras. B-D).

Obviously, the role of the Receiver/Manager is similar to that of a director who is in a fiduciary position. Such Receiver has a duty of care and the receiver/managers must have requisite experience to leverage on their knowledge and expertise in dealing with the debtor company's assets.His duties being rooted in rules of equity, the Receiver-Manager must not accept secret profits.[223]He must avoid conflict of interest, duty abdication or *mala fides*. Thus, unwholesome benefits and transactions are voidable by the aggrieved party who may seek remedies like restitution to the debtor company, prosecution for criminal breach of trust and damages.[224]

5. *The Procedure and Effects of Winding-Up Proceedings under the AMCON Act*

By definition, winding-up is the process of settling accounts and liquidating assets in anticipation of a dissolution of a partnership or company whilst bankruptcy proceedings are specialised legal proceedings employed by either a creditor (to recover his exposure to a debtor) or a debtor (to obtain financial reliefs, by means of judicial process, from his debtors). Consequently, while winding-up proceedings are initiated against a company, bankruptcy proceedings are against individuals.

Statutorily, section 52 of the AMCON Act grants special powers to AMCON to make an application for the winding-up of a debtor company where there is a court decision against a body corporate in a debt recovery action requiring such company to pay some money to AMCON and the debtor company fails to liquidate the debt within 90 days after the order is made.[225]

S. 52 thereof states;

> *"where the court gives a decision against a body corporate, in a debt/recovery action under this Act, requiring the debtor company to pay any sum to the corporation and such sum is not liquidated or paid over to the corporation within 90 days from the date of the order for payment, the corporation may apply to the court to issue a winding up order against the debtor company."*

Furthermore, the Court may appoint the Official Receiver or some other fit person as a Liquidator to wind up the affairs of the debtor Company. Such Liquidator shall have all the powers of a Liquidator under CAMA and must discharge his duties, accordingly.

The effect of the Winding-Up order is that the liquidator appointed by the court collects the assets of the company, including uncalled capital on shares, and

---

[223] Section 87 CAMA
[224]Section 311 of the Penal Code
[225]Tonique Oil Services Limited v. Asset Management Corporation of Nigeria (2018) LPELR-45106(CA)

pays the creditors in order of priority. The Liquidator then will distribute any surplus funds to the shareholders prior to the formal dissolution of the company.

Specifically, section 51 of the AMCON Act also grants special powers to AMCON to file bankruptcy proceedings based on the following grounds:

a. Existence of a Court decision against a debtor (an individual in this case);
b. The decision must be given in a debt-recovery action;
c. The decision requires the debtor to pay AMCON a sum of money; and
d. The judgement sum has not been paid or liquidated within 30 days of the date of the order for payment.

Undercurrent AMCON regime, the debtor need not have committed any act of bankruptcy, for AMCON to file a bankruptcy petition, or for any of the conditions precedent for the grant of a receiving order specified under the Bankruptcy Act to exist. The judge is given power at any time to grant the receiving Order and to also declare the debtor bankrupt.

The consequence of a receiving order is that the debtor's properties become immediately divisible among his creditors and vests in the trustee appointed by the Court.[226] The trustee or Committee of Inspection (as the case may be) shall be responsible for disposing the debtor's properties and settling the claims of the creditors in order of priority.

Although, winding up proceedings are not legally and conceptually meant to be instruments of debt recovery,[227] nevertheless, the process presents itself as an effective tool in debt recovery under the AMCON Act. The special powers granted to AMCON under Section 52 of the AMCON Act have greatly reduced the stretch of the procedure and the time spent in Winding-Up proceedings and enforcing debt recovery judgements.

Furthermore, where a debtor company is undergoing winding-up proceedings and a liquidator has been appointed, there is no assurance that all the debts owed by the company would be recovered.[228] In practice, the preferential claims under s. 494 CAMA take a large part of the realised funds, and AMCON may only realise the leftover after a payment to the preferential claim holders.

In bankruptcy proceedings, the directors and shareholders may be faced with bankruptcy proceedings where they are personally liable for debts. Section 60 of the AMCON Act defines "debtor" and "Debtor Company" to include the Director. Hence, in a situation where AMCON obtains judgement in a debt-recovery action against a company and discovers that a director has embezzled

---

[226] Section 20, 21 and 22 of the Bankruptcy Act, Cap B2 LFN, 2004
[227] See Oriental Airlines Ltd vs. Air Via Ltd. (1998) 12 NWLR (Pt. 577) 271 at 280-281, (2004) LEPLR-272(SC), Nigeria Industrial Development Bank Ltd. Vs. Fembo Nigeria Limited (1997), (2010)LPELR-8965(CA)
[228] Section 494 CAMA

some funds in relation to the debt, AMCON may proceed against such director in a bankruptcy proceeding.

This provision enables AMCON to side track the stringent provisions of sections 18 – 22 of the Bankruptcy Act which requires that the trustee or Receiver-manager have free control in discharging his responsibility. Committee of inspection, even in cases of schemes of composition and arrangement being made by the Creditor.

6. An Overview of the Federal High Court ADR Rules
    i.   Scope

The Federal High Court (Alternative Dispute Resolution) Rules, (FHC-ADR Rules) 2018 is a Court-Connected ADR (CCADR) procedure which makes the utilisation of ADR as an essential pre-trial process at the instance of a judge of the FHC in deserving cases. Order 5 of the ADR Rules uses the word "shall" in the opening paragraph of the Rule making ADR mandatory in the FHC. Nonetheless, this compulsory approach does not necessarily precipitate an abdication of judicial duties by the court.

However, the FHC-ADR Rules expand the provisions of Order 18 of the extant Civil Procedure Rules of the Federal High Court which encourage settlement of civil disputes as much as possible within thirty (30) days[229]. "When a matter comes before the Court for the first time, the judge shall, in circumstances where it is appropriate, grant to the parties, time not more than thirty (30) days within which parties may explore possibilities for settlement of the disputes." Order 18 of the extant FHC Rules makes a reference to ADR encouraging out-of-court settlement without any detailed procedure and the ADR mechanisms that may be adopted.

    ii.   Objectives of the FHC-ADR Rules 2018

The FHC Rules establish a Dispute Resolution Centre as a department of the FHC[230] to administer core ADR mechanisms with the following key objectives stated under *Order 1 Rule 1(1) (a) & (b)* which are:

i.   *To enhance access to justice by providing alternative mechanisms to supplement litigation in the resolution of disputes.*

ii.   *To minimize frustration/delays in justice delivery by promoting standard procedural framework for fair and efficient settlement of disputes through alternative dispute resolution mechanisms[231].*

iii.   *To provide for a focal point for the promotion of ADR in Court.*

iv.   *To promote the growth and effective functioning of the justice system through ADR mechanisms.*

---

[229] Order 18 Rule (1)
[230] Order 2(1) of the FHC (ADR) Rules
[231] See Order 1 Rule 1(1)(a)&(b) of the FHC-ADR Rules. 2018.

By virtue of *Order 1 Rule 3,* the ADR Rules set out the application of mediation, conciliation, arbitration, neutral evaluation and any other ADR mechanisms in the resolution of disputes referred to the Centre from the Court.[232] The centre works as a Department of the Federal High Court with court connected ADR venue and offices located within the premises of the Court or any other suitable locations that may be approved by the Chief Judge of the Court. The ADR Rules seem to function like court-ordered proceedings and not to have a life of their own. This is a departure from the Lagos Multi door Court (LMDC) in Lagos State where parties can opt to file directly at the LMDC.

Under Order 8(1)(2)(3)(4) of the FHC-ADR Rules, 2018, ADR Sessions are private and confidential. All evidence is disclosed or made on a "without prejudice" basis and no privilege or confidentiality shall be deemed to have been waived by such disclosure. This is contrasted with the Evidence Act, which has granted certain privileges.

iii.   Jurisdictional Issues under AMCON Act 2010 (as amended):

The Federal High Court is the only court vested with jurisdiction over AMCON claims under S. 61 of the AMCON Act. Under s.53 thereof, the Chief Judge of the Federal High Court designates a Judge for recovery of AMCON debts i.e. (Special Debt recovery procedure). Under s. 48 thereof, the Chief Judge has the power to Act as or appoint a receiver whilst s.50 grants the Court the power to attach or freeze accounts of debtors. Provisions for compromise forgiveness and settlement are stated under section 6 (1) (i) and 6 (5) of the Act.

Accordingly, AMCON Practice Direction 2013 (Federal High Court) Special debt recovery procedure provides as follows[233]:

> *"The Chief Judge of the Federal High Court may designate any Judge of the Federal High Court to hear matters for the recovery of debts owed to the Corporation or an eligible financial institution and other matters arising from the provisions of this Act to the exclusion of any other matter for such period as may be determined by the Chief Judge".*

7. The Scope of Sections 49 & 50 of the AMCON ACT

The scope, application and limitation of sections 49 & 50 of the AMCON Act were extensively considered by the Court of Appeal[234]. The court held that section 49 of the Act gives the Appellant power to approach the courts for an order to protect the assets of an AMCON debtor whom AMCON reasonably believes were about to dissipate assets and that the order can be made as a precursor to an action. Accordingly, ss. 49 & 50 cannot be applied when the parties have already joined issues before the court in the same subject matter. The Court expressed the opinion that once the parties have invoked the

---

[232]By Order 1 Rule 3 of the FHC (ADR) Rules
[233]section 53 AMCON Act
[234]AMCON v Bi-Courtney &Ors. APPEAL NO. CA/L/930/14 delivered on 25th Day of March, 2015

jurisdiction of the court, it is the court that is seized of the matter as the appropriate forum for resolving the dispute between the parties. Consequentially, section 49 and section 50 cannot be invoked to create another forum for the ventilation of the issues where the parties have already joined issues in court.

> "... The provisions of Section 49 of the Act are just designed to serve the purpose of mareva injunction in civil actions. The Section is primarily meant to serve the Corporation in its aggressive pursuit of loans recovery, and prevent recalcitrant debtors from dissipating collateral or other assets, pending the conclusion of recovery proceedings, it certainly does not and will never serve as a vehicle for the corporation to engage in stealing a match against a party in litigation. Once there is an existing suit in respect of the subject matter, and parties are properly constituted before a court the provisions of Section 49 will not be available to the Corporation..."[235]

8. The Court of Appeal (Fast Track) Practice Direction 2014

The Court of Appeal (Fast Track) Practice Direction 2014 is a tool against recalcitrant debtors who use Stay of proceedings pending interlocutory appeals to protract proceedings. Also, oral address is allowed under Order 8, Rule 8.The Direction discourages interlocutory appeals and requires parties, except in deserving cases, to subsume their interlocutory matters under a final appeal under the substantive suit at the trial".

9. Conclusions
a. Progressively, AMCON has been given extensive powers and support to minimise the debt overhang by creditor banks.
b. Various traditional remedies have been useful in the recovery process as well as new modalities to trace assets of chronic debtors.
c. Undoubtedly, the winding up regime under the CAMA is special augment inadequate.
d. The ADR process under AMCON has been institutionalised to achieve quicker recovery process to forestall or minimise corrupt breaches of prudential guidelines issued by regulatory authorities.

10. Recommendations
a. The Courts are encouraged to invoke section 25(2) of the Mortgage Law of Lagos State on Eligible Bank Assets (EBAs) secured by the debtor depositing the fund if applicable for injunction to be granted when power of sale is to be exercised.
b. At the Appellate level, the Rules of Court should be amended to incorporate Fast Track Practice Direction 2014 to ensure strict compliance with Case Management.

---

[235]Tanzilla Petroleum Co. Ltd & Anor v. AMCON. 2017 LPELR-42986 (CA). Mareva Campania Naviera S.A. V International Bulcaneers (SA) 1975 2 Lloyds Rep 500

c. There is need for greater promotion of alternative dispute resolution mechanisms such as mediation as effective vehicle for expeditious resolution of issues between AMCON and its debtors.
d. The courts should impose heavy costs to discourage frivolous and vexatious litigations aimed at derailing quick debt recovery.
e. The causes of action that qualify for ADR should be specified in the ADR Rules.
f. The Law should craft more rules for holding in-house staff of financial institutions liable in tort or otherwise collaborations in breaching banking prudential guidelines.

Recent ADR Issues in the Recovery of Debts in Nigeria*

Abstract

Finance has been the life blood of business even before the landmark case of Salomon v Salomon Ltd (1897). Thus, various legislations provide for security of properties, foreclosure, power of sale of creditors assets, liquidation/winding-up and appointment of receiver managers in case of default in loan payment. As a relief, foreclosure is usually pursued by mortgagors acquiring the mortgaged property free from the mortgagors' equity of redemption. However, obligors/debtors of Banks still continue to devise strategies to either prolong recovery actions by way of technical defences or other practices to frustrate recoveries.

A 2019 release by the CBN revealed that the level of Non-Performing Loans (NPLs) within the Nigerian banking system was still high at N1.5 trillion recording 15% increase over previous year which results in low level of liquidity in banks, increased threat of bank failures, threat of financial sector crises and ultimately threat to democracy and the national economy. Due to the slow judicial process in Nigeria and also for greater efficiency in the recovery of debts, AMCON was established in 2011 mainly to enable banks focus on their core mandate of advancing credit to build the economy rather than pursuing recovery of bad or doubtful debts. Recently, the Federal High Court followed up the move for faster recovery process and established the Federal High Court (Alternative Dispute Resolution) Rules, 2018 (The FHC-ADR Rules) with effect from the 13th day of December 2018. ADR is widely known as usually less expensive, fast, simple and flexible by which creditors would rather not seek full recovery of reimbursement as opposed to settlements or compromise of the indebtedness by other judicial means and self-help process.

The FHC-ADR Rules expand the provisions of Order 18 of the extant Civil Procedure Rules of the Federal High Court which encourage settlement of civil disputes as much as possible within thirty (30) days. Order 18 Rule (1) states "When a matter comes before the Court for the first time, the judge shall, in circumstances where it is appropriate, grant to the parties, time not more than thirty (30) days within which parties may explore possibilities for settlement of the disputes." Notably, Order 18, thereof makes a reference to the use of ADR, in passing, which encourages out-of-court settlement without any detailed procedure of the ADR mechanisms that may be adopted. A purposive interpretation of the rules, made in passing, assumes encouragement of ADRs rather than abdication by the courts of their duties.

1. Definition of Terms

Alternative Dispute Regulation (ADR) essentially refers to various procedures for settling disputes as an alternative to litigation in the court of law. The ADR process involves the intervention and/or assistance of a neutral and impartial third party and has the following main features. viz:

a) Voluntariness or absence of compulsion
b) Confidential
c) Thrives on party good faith and willingness to compromise
d) Usually backed by an agreement of Parties
e) Flexibility
f) Largely party-driven
g) Non-compulsively binding (except arbitration) but not self-enforcing.

2. Kinds of ADR under the Rules are;
a) Early Neutral Evaluation (ENE):
  ➢ In this model, an expert gives opinion on the strengths and weaknesses of parties' evidence and arguments. The decision is not usually binding but merely a basis for negotiation.

b) Negotiation;
  ➢ By this process, two or more parties, directly or through representatives bargain on their competing interests.
  ➢ No third party is used as facilitator
  ➢ The process usually paves the way for a mutually acceptable resolution

c) Mediator/Conciliation
  ➢ This involves structured discussions before a 3rd neutral/impartial arbiter is invited to facilitate between the parties
  ➢ The role of the neutral person hardly goes beyond exploring avenues for settlement. The mediator normally plays a more active role in ensuring a settlement is reached.

d) Med-Arb
  ➢ This is a two-tiered process which commences with mediation, failing which parties go to arbitration
  ➢ The final result becomes binding and enforceable as in arbitration

e) Expert Determination
  ➢ This involves an expert applying his special skill to determine a dispute fairly
  ➢ The Expert does not act judicially, but must exhibit fairness
  ➢ This form is commonly used in industry disputes e.g. construction, oil & gas etc.

f) Arbitration

> ➢ Parties refer a dispute by an express or implied ***agreement,*** to an ***impartial*** private tribunal of ***choice*** for resolution by way of a ***legal binding decision***
> ➢ A binding decision is one of the most distinguished elements of arbitration in distinction to other ADR forms
> ➢ Arbitrations are not self-enforcing and enforcement is through the courts. Thus, the cooperation and supervision of the Courts' are usually involved.

The objectives of the Rules of the Federal High Court are as follows[236]:

a. Enhance access to justice by providing alternative mechanisms to supplement litigation in the resolution of disputes;
b. Minimise frustration and delays in justice delivery by providing a standard procedural framework for the fair and efficient settlement of disputes through alternative dispute resolution (ADR) mechanisms;
c. Provide for a focal point for the promotion of ADR in the Court; and
d. Promote the growth and effective functioning of the justice system through ADR mechanisms.

A dispute resolution centre was set up for the Court, viz[237];

1. The Centre shall be a –
   a. Department of the Court; and
   b. Court-connected ADR venue, with its offices located within the premises of the Court and any other suitable locations as may be approved by the Chief Judge.
2. The Centre shall –
   a. Apply mediation, conciliation, arbitration, neutral evaluation and any other ADR mechanisms in the resolution of disputes, as may from time to time be referred to it, from the Court;
   b. Encourage disputing parties to appear before it for the resolution of their disputes;
   c. Act as an administrator in the conduct of the ADR proceedings;
   d. Publicize its activities by informing and sensitizing the public about its facilities.
   e. Render assistance to disputing parties, in the conduct of ad-hoc arbitration or mediation proceedings;
   f. Encourage disputing parties whose matters are already filed before the Court to explore ADR options at the Centre;
   g. Maintain registers of suitably qualified persons who can act as mediators, arbitrators or neutral evaluators; and

---

[236] Order 1 of the Rules
[237] Order 2, Ditto

h. Promote or undertake projects or other activities including an "ADR Awareenss Week" which will further assist in decongesting the Court and help to achive the purpose for which the Centre was established.

3. – (1) The Director of the Centre shall submit to the Chief Judge of the Court, quarterly reports or for such period as the Chief Judge may require, detailing the activities of the Centre during the period under review and containing statistics of cases, trends and patterns, notable observation and challenges encountered in the course of implementing the objective of the Centre.

(2) the Director of the Centre shall submit annual reports to the ADR Committee.

Under Order 2, the centre shall be under the supervision of the ADR Committee (in these Rules referred to as "the Committee")

The Committee shall –

a. consider and approve the annual budget of the Centre;
b. consider the annual report of the Centre;
c. initiate or validate proposals to restructure and expand the Centre;
d. foster the relationship between the Centre and other private or government establishments; and
e. perform other functions as the Committee may consider appropriate for the overall development and growth of the Centre and to enhance the effective administration and speedy delivery of justice.

1. (1) The Committee shall consist of –
a. The Chief Judge of the Court;
b. Two badges of the Court appointed by the Chief Judge;
c. The Chief Registrar of the Court;
d. A representative of the Federal Ministry of Justice, nominated by the Attorney General of the Federation; etc.

4. *Recording Disputes in the ADR Register/Time Limit for Dispute Resolution*

The ADR Centre requires the establishment of a Register of Disputes for cases. A case officer is required to assist disputants.[238] The maximum time allowed for parties to explore ADR is sixty (60) days from the date of the referral of the dispute to the ADR Centre.[239] However, the court, before which the substantive matter is pending, may extend the length of time by a period of not more than 30 days upon an application by the Centre with the consent of all parties.[240]

---

[238] Order 6 Rule 1 of the Federal High Court (Alternative Dispute Resolution) Rules, 2018 (FHC ADR Rules).
[239] Order 6 Rule 5
[240] Ibid, FHC-ADR Rules 2018

Furthermore, when a matter is initiated before the court the judge shall in appropriate[241]_ circumstances grant to the parties, time of not more than 21 days within which parties may explore possibilities for settlement of the dispute.[242] Thus, all AMCON cases pending before the Federal High Court are subject to the Federal High Court ADR Initiative.

Appointment of an arbitrator is not governed by or provided for under CAMA but by the Arbitration and Conciliation Act Cap 19 of the Laws of the Federation, 1990 and falls outside s. 25(1)(e) of the 1999 Constitution.

The duty of an arbitrator chosen by agreement of the parties is to settle any dispute between the parties. A receiver on the other hand is appointed to administer in the company or property in question.

3. Enforcement of decisions of the ADR Centre

Upon the completion of a dispute resolution, settlement agreements, duly signed by the parties, shall be enforceable as a contract between the parties and deemed to be enforceable under section 25 of the Arbitration and Conciliation Act.[243] Similarly, where the ADR process terminates in an Arbitral Award, the decision shall be enforced as provided for in the Arbitration and Conciliation Act. This principle is reinforced by Order 10 Rule 2 of the Federal High Court (Alternative Dispute Resolution) Rules, 2018.[244]

In cases of loan syndication where there are two or more lenders which may be secured or non-secured, the issue of priority in the settlement of the loans in the event of default naturally may arise. The complexities which loan syndication presents sometimes take time and the multiplicity of parties could create diverse problems in ADR especially when each of the parties may insist on established and entrenched rights in the loan documentation.

The LMDC has been effective in resolving credit disputes most of which relate to over charged interest rates or domiciliation without charge or mortgage, particularly where it is shown that both the bank and the debtor are committed to a long term mutual beneficial interest or are still desirous of preserving long term relationships.

Some vitiating elements in utilising ADR for recovery have arisen where some bad loans have been found to possess some attributes like misrepresentation, forged collaterals or non-existent borrowers usually with the collusion of in-house bank officers or officers at the Land Registry). In the event of default, such frauds have constituted major impediments and defence to the loan

---

[241] Order 11, Rule 1 of the Federal High Court (Asset Management Corporation of Nigeria) Proceedings Rules

[242] The Federal High Court (Asset Management Corporation of Nigeria) Proceedings Rules, 2018 were issued by the Honourable Chief Judge of the Federal High Court, Adamu A. Kefarati on the 13th December, 2018.

[243] Order 10 Rule 1(a)&(b) (FHC) ADR Rules, 2018

[244] Order 10 Rule 2 (FHC) ADR Rules, 2018

enforcement and parties have been reluctant to use the ADR mechinery. Apart from using state security enforcement apparatus such as the Economic and Financial Crimes Commission (EFCC) or the police, some parties insist on prosecution in addition to civil remedies in court as opposed to ADR.

4. The Wide Scope of AMCON's Powers and Duties.

Under s. 48 of the AMCON Act, extensive powers were granted AMCON in order to effectively exercise its core mandate which include the following:

- Purchase the toxic and bad loans from commercial banks and remove them from the balance sheet of the banks.
- Return the banks to liquidity to preserve and protect Depositors' funds.
- Aggressive pursuit of the recovery of debts purchased.
- Acquisition, purchase or otherwise holding, managing, realising and disposing of Eligible Bank Assets (EBA);
- Performing functions directly relating to the management or realization of Eligible Bank Assets (EBAs); and
- Taking all steps necessary or expedient to protect the assets.

Furthermore, AMCON's core duties were spelt out under s. 48 and specifically include as follows[245]:

- Assist eligible financial institutions to efficiently dispose of eligible bank assets (EBAs) in accordance with the provisions of the Act;
- Efficiently manage and dispose of eligible bank assets acquired by AMCON in accordance with the provisions of the Act; and
- Obtain the best achievable financial returns on Eligible Bank Assets (EBAs) or other assets acquired by it in pursuance of the provisions of the Act having regard to
  - The need to protect or otherwise enhance the long-term economic value of those assets;
  - The cost of acquiring and dealing with those assets;
  - AMCON's cost of capital and other costs;
  - Any guidelines or directions issued by the Central Bank of Nigeria in pursuance of the provisions of the Act; and
  - Any other factors which AMCON considers relevant to the achievement of its objectives.

Also, other statutory provisions like the Conveyancing Act of 1881 and the 2010 Mortgage and Property Law of Lagos State all confer similar rights on creditors to take possession even if there is no express provision in the loan instruments. Likewise, sections 49(1) and 50(1) of the AMCON Act confer special powers on AMCON to take possession of immovable assets of a debtor and also to freeze

---

[245] Section 4 of the AMCON Act as amended,

the account of debtor in accordance with the common law approach to protect creditor's investment from dissipation.

As a secured creditor AMCON derives its Powers of Sale and foreclosure of the mortgaged property statutorily and contractually once the legal or contractual date of redemption has passed. If the debt is payable by instalments, the power of sale arises as soon as any instalment is in arrears[246].

In addition, under Section 48(1) of the AMCON Act, the Corporation has the power to act as, or appoint a receiver for a debtor company whose assets have been charged, mortgaged or pledged as security for an eligible bank asset acquired by the Corporation. Thus, two types of Receivers may be appointed under the AMCON Act namely:

- o AMCON itself may act as a receiver or a
- o Receiver may be appointed under the AMCON Act[247].

Where the Non Performing Loan forming the eligible bank assets is unsecured and not collateralised, the remedial power of AMCON is the right to pursue the debtor to recover the loans as an unsecured creditor. However, where AMCON is a Secured Creditor the corporation has the following salient powers:

- to take possession
- to Appoint a Receiver
- to sell the secured Asset
- to Foreclose the Asset
- freeze Accounts of the debtor company

5. Some essential features of the AMCON Practice Direction 2013, Court of Appeal Practice Direction, 2014.

For speedy conclusion of ADRs, the Courts' Case Management Rules provide for identification of issues for investigation/trial, use of technology, consolidation and acceleration of proceedings. Also, at trial, the Court must seek to minimise, curtail abusive, aggressive or excessive cross examination under Part V. Specifically, achievement of speed and efficiency in court proceedings are provided and encouraged as goals. Thus, the Court may sit from day to day, every week day and on Saturday.[248]

Also, it is provided in the Practice Direction that court vacation does not apply to AMCON and Interim Remedies may be provided under Part III: e.g. trial and addresses must be concluded within 3 months, and Judgement to be given within 21 days or as soon as possible but must not exceed 90 days; judgements can be

---

[246] S. 120(1); s. 19(1), s. 35(1) PCL
[247] Prince Abdul Raheed A.. & Anor, Adetona v Zenith International Bank Ltd (2007) LPELR-8896 (CA), SC 78/2007; Magbagbeola v. Sanni (2005) 11 NWLR (Pt. 936) 239; (2005) 4 FWLR Part 279, p. 237.Intercontractors v. NPFMB (1988)2 NWLR Part 76, p. 280.
[248] Para 5.1

possession or freezing of creditors assets, injunction, declaration, Mareva, Anton Piller arrest of absconding defendants.

6. Conclusions

a. It is crucial for the debt recovery process to be more effective so that the nation's resources can be circulated for the common good, instead of being concentrated in the hands of few Nigerians.

b. Decisions of courts which offend the laudable objectives of arbitration discourage parties from submission to ADR to thereby delaying funds for commercial uses and national development[249]. Arbitral awards may only be set aside for Error of law[250].

c. ADRs are more difficult to administer in syndicated loan transactions. The presence of fraud or vitiating elements of criminality tends to complicate ADR. However, parties should desist from using state security agencies for debt recovery and should rely on authentic Land Registry documents.

d. Professional and well educated receivers have more capacity to navigate ADR by applying knowledge during discussions and negotiations to achieve effective repayment plans and realise assets.

e. Dedication of special courts by the Federal high Court to deal with AMCON related matters like the Commercial Courts Division in Lagos State is salutary and should be enhanced.

f. More astute efforts in the recovery of debts will minimise the poor attitude and temerity of many chronic debtors to unduly prolong recoveries.

---

[249] The Shell Petroleum Development Company of Nigeria Limited & 2 Ors. v Crestar Integrated Natural Resources Limited. (2016) 9NWLR (Pt. 1517) P.300
[250] Escaliber Ventures LL.C v Texas Keystone In; Taylor Woodrow (Nig.) Ltd. (1993) 4NWLR Part 286 All E.R (Comm) 933; Champsey Bhara & Co. V Jivrays Balloo Spinning & Weaving Co. (1923) AC 480, 2015 LWELLLR-40034(CA).

Salient Developments and Challenges in Enforcing Judgement Debts

Abstract

On a global scale, economies have continued to suffer sudden crashes and chronic economic diseases, as when trillion dollar dud mortgages blew up the financial system in 2007/8. Expectedly, the United States government intervened to buoy the two (2) giant mortgage companies of Fanny Mac and Freddie Mac to support business and the economy. In this wise, the Nigerian government has recently bailed out banks deemed too big to fail because of systemic collapses as was the case in Skye Bank/Polaris Bank. In Nigeria, non-performing loans have peaked at about N10 trillion by 2020. Bank liquidations do not guarantee quick realisation of assets of insured depositors and creditors but are the last recourses by regulatory systems to minimise disruptions. Globally, cross border trade finances are growing with the Belt and Silk Initiative. Recognition and enforcement of insolvency are coming to the fore in the highest courts on a regular basis, giving way to modified universalism in jurisdictional processes. These trajectories have been interrogated to present the need for a harmonisation and consolidation of the rules of insolvency, bankruptcy and winding up of companies for certainty by legal community. In doing that, the various challenges to debt enforcement in Nigeria and beyond have been analysed and reviews advocated.

I. Introduction

Usually, the mode of enforcement of a judgement depends largely upon the type of judgement in question. In *Government of Gongola State v Tukur*[251]*,* the Supreme Court listed the methods of enforcing different kinds of judgement as follows:

i. A judgement or order for payment of money may be enforced by a Writ of fieri facias, garnishee proceedings, a charging order, a writ of sequestration or an order for committal on judgement debtor's summons;

ii. A judgement for possession of land may be enforced by a writ of possession, a writ of sequestration or committal order,

---

*Kathleen Okafor, Baze University, Abuja. Ke_okafor@yahoo.com
[251] (1989) LPELR SC 148/88, 1989 A.N.L.R 575

iii. A judgement for delivery of goods may be enforced by a writ of specific delivery or restitution of their value, a writ of sequestration or writ of committal.

iv. A judgement restraining the doing of an act may be enforced by an order of committal or a writ of sequestration against the property of the disobedient person.

In the case of**Rubin v Euro Finance**[252]and others, the Appellants appealed to the Supreme Court against the Court of Appeal judgement in favour of David Rubin and Henry Lan (Respondent), the receivers and managers of The Consumers Trust (TCT). The case concerned an English law governed trustwhich was the repository of funds raised through a cash back program run by the Appellants. The program ran into financial difficulties and was sued by various Attorney-Generals in the US who sought Chapter 11 protection in the Southern District of New York. The court gave a default judgement against the Appellants who did not attend the proceedings believing that by not attending they were not subject to that court's jurisdiction.

The Respondents sought to enforce the judgement in England pursuant to the Cross Border Insolvency Regulations (CBIR), 2006. The court first instance refused to enforce it on the basis that the CBIR did not cover enforcement. The Court of Appeal allowed enforcement under the common law. The court of Appeal accepted Lord Hoffman's comments in the Privy Council case of *Cambridge Gas Transportation Corporation v Official Committee of Unsecured Creditors of Navigator Holdings Plc.*[253] where the idea of universalism in bankruptcy, was promoted meaning that a bankruptcy judgement could be enforced automatically even though it might otherwise be classified as an action in personam judgement subject to the ordinary rules of Private International Law, as set out at Rule 36 of Dicey, Morris and Collins[254], that national courts will apply the rules of procedures of their courts.

Upholding the Judgement of the Court of Appeal, for enforcement under the CBIR, the Supreme Court agreed that bankruptcy judgements are to be treated as a separate category of judgement which otherwise will be tantamount to hundreds of overturning years of accepted jurisprudence. Although salutary for insolvency and restructuring practitioners and insolvency lawyers in England, the judgement could increase financial penalties on those who have dealt with insolvent companies and who may now have to attend hearings all over the world to defend their actions.

Another interesting case has been the Integrated Medical Solution Ltd(IMS)[255]. In October 2011, in proceedings taking place across Ireland and England, an

---

[252] (2012) U.K. SC 46
[253][2006] UKPC 26; 2013 BCC 1
[254] Dicey, Morris & Collins on the Conflict of Laws 15th edn. Books, - Practical Law, Thomson Reuters
[255]

Irish company secured unique cooperation between the Irish and English courts in relation to the examiner ship of a group of companies, resulting in the Irish High Court granting protection to a UK company under Irish examiner ship law. The first-ever successful application was made for:

- court protection in Ireland for an insolvent UK company under the Irish Companies (Amendment) Act 1990; and
- The dismissal of a winding-up petition in the UK based on a letter from the Irish High court and assistance under the Cross-Border Insolvency Regulations.

II. Challenges of Enforcement:

Usually, attempts by creditors to realize securities or mortgages due to the mortgagors' defaults have been met with difficulties. Creditors resort to self-help as a means of realizing their security by entering the mortgagors' premises to distrain goods, chattels, cars and cash, yatchs. Usually, mortgagees also apply general rights of lien created by mortgagees over the security of the mortgage and other goods of the mortgagors.

To forestall deteriorating lawlessness, also occasioned by uncertainties in the law and delays in the process, the right to self-help has however been criminalised in Enugu State of Nigeria and as such it no longer avails the mortgagee [256]. In the case of *Richard Ozobu v C.C.B. Plc.* [257]. The plaintiff/applicants claimed the right against the defendant bank at the Enugu High Court to declare that the attempt by the defendant to realise the mortgage by way of self-help was void because the mortgage under the deed was to be repaid in twenty years beginning from 1994 but in 1995 the mortgagee attempted to realize the mortgage contrary to the terms of the mortgage by impounding the cars and cash of the mortgagor. The plaintiff/mortgagor also sought an interlocutory injunction. The court stated that:

> Where an order granting liberty to sell a mortgage property has lapsed, the mortgagee needs another court order to validly sell the property after a demand. In the instant case, the order to attach had expired and no longer valid. It could not invoke the power of sale directly.

Furthermore, lame submissions by recalcitrant debtors and has been a great challenge to loan/mortgage recovery. Thus, where a guarantor has fully repaid a creditor, such guarantor is clearly entitled to recover the debt paid from the principal debtor. The guarantor automatically stands in the creditor's shoes, having satisfied the debt. This position was confirmed in *Beloxxi & Company Ltd & Anor v South Trust Bank & Ors* [258], where the 1ST Appellant obtained a loan of $2,207,600.00 from the 1st Respondent, with the 2nd Respondent as

---

[256] Richard Ozobu v C.C.B. Plc (unreported) Suit No. E/246/95
[257] Ibid
[258](2014) LPELR-22338

Guarantor. When the 1st Appellant defaulted, the 2nd Respondent repaid the loan and stepped into the shoes of the 1st Respondent to claim the money from the 1st Appellant.

A different challenge was experienced by the mortgagees in the case of *South Trust Bank & Ors v Pheanzy Gas Limited & Ors*[259]. The 1st respondent borrowed $4,420,091.00 from the 1st and 3rd Appellant, with the 2nd appellant as guarantor. When the 1st respondent defaulted, the 2nd appellant was to repay and step into the shoes of the 1st and 3rd Appellants, and recover the loan from the respondents. The 1st respondent defaulted, and the 2nd Appellant repaid the loans, and obtained an assignment of the loans. The 2nd Appellant demanded repayment but the Respondents responded with a suit at the trial court. As a primary issue, the trial court found that the respondents were liable to repay the loan. The trial court held that the proper venue for litigation of the counterclaim was New York. The Court of Appeal saved the appellant mortagees the hardship of the case being remitted to a lower court for rehearing.

III. The common law and modified universalism

In the UK, the Insolvency Act of 1986 is the key legislation while the Insolvency Rules 1986 govern the procedure. Due to globalisation, many insolvencies now involve cross-border insolvencies which need to be reconciled in different jurisdictions to provide swift and effective remedies to combat the use of cross-border transfers of assets to evade and defraud creditors. The choice of jurisdictional process of territorialism allows each jurisdiction to act with regard to assets within its jurisdiction while universalism provides for one jurisdiction to assume responsibility for all the assets and liabilities wherever located. A modified universalism involves identifying the jurisdiction best placed to deal with the insolvent entity while recognising the sovereign right of other jurisdictions to manage aspects of the insolvency process within their territories in respect of assets and liabilities located there. In *Singularis Holdings Ltd v PricewaterhouseCoopers*[260], LordMance expatiated on the very essence of modified universalism consisting in the recognition by the courts of the foreign liquidator's power of disposition of the company's assets in the domestic jurisdiction which justifies an order restraining their disposition or seizure inconsistent with that foreign liquidation.

The exact extent of modified universalism in Nigeria remains inconclusive. However, in the United States, the Supreme Court clearly avoided adoption of clear universalism when[261] it refused a request by a receiver of a US company to enforce in the UK, a US default judgement with respect to transactions which were either an undervalue or a preference against defendants. Applying ordinary principles of private international law (the Dicey rule), the judgement could not

---

[259] (2014) JELR-47019(CA)
[260] (2014) UK PC 36
[261] Rubin v Eurofinance SA (2012) UK SC 46

be enforced in the UK in those circumstances. The court held that the principle of modified universalism did not override those rules to require the English courts to give recognition to judgements in foreign insolvency proceedings.

Also, the Privy Council by a 3-2 majority rejected an application by the liquidators appointed in the Cayman Islands that the courts of Bermuda make an order directing a company's auditor to disclose information to the liquidators[262]. There was the issue of whether the power of disclosure which the liquidators wanted the Bermunda court to exercise was not a power of disclosure which existed in the Cayman Islands so the order could not have been obtained by the liquidators in their home jurisdiction.

The EC Regulation on Insolvency Proceedings (Council Regulation (EC) No. 1346/2000) has attempted to address the concerns on universalism in order to improve the efficiency and effectiveness of insolvency proceedings which have cross-border effect.

In summary, the regulation provides that where territorial proceedings are commenced after the opening of main proceedings, the proceedings will be treated as secondary proceedings and, under the Regulation they must be winding up rather than rescue proceedings.

Remarkably, the objective of the Regulation is to simplify access of foreign representatives and creditors to the courts and insolvency procedures of Great Britain which are particularly valuable in the context of UK/US insolvencies. The Model Law entitles a foreign representative to apply directly to the courts to commence insolvency proceedings and to participate in such proceedings as well as provide for the recognition of the foreign proceedings, Foreign representatives may also be involved in the co-ordination of proceedings concerning the same debtor, rights of foreign creditors, the rights and duties of foreign representatives and co-operation between national authorities.

IV. Conclusions& Recommendations
1. Due to globalisation of capital and trade, there is need for greater harmonisation of bankruptcy, insolvency rules and the procedures for debt recovery to minimise uncertainty as to the proper legal recourse.
2. Receivers and managers should be better regulated and organised under a uniform professional body for regulatory and professional conduct to ensure that suppliers of capital do not face forum shopping and other impediments to universal availability of cross border capital for business development.
3. The Courts must be constantly in collaboration with policy makers and law enforcement agencies in the maintenance of high standards of international best practices of corporate governance and debt repayment schedules.

---

[262]*Singularis Holdings Ltd v PricewaterCoopers, Supra.*

4. Continuous enlightenment of lawyers, judges, shareholders and fund managers is critical for greater understanding of the adjudicatory options in debt recovery.
5. Corporate stakeholders should always consider the option of ADR to quickly resolve disputes amicably for business continuity.

SOME DEVELOPMENTS OF DEBTS PERSPECTIVES

1. BACKGROUND

Men, have tried to provide sufficiency and surplus through the request for loans. However, economic and political structures have hampered the realization of the initiatives towards borrowing. This paper has sought to examine the macro and definition of terms in order to make recommendations for more egalitarian societies.

INTRODUCTION:

Whether in Marxist, socialist or capitalist system, commerce has been eponymous to debt. The necessity to collect debts existed long before currency was invented. The bartering of goods or services in return for other goods or services often led to the creation of debt as one of the parties failed sometimes to deliver their goods or services, as agreed.

A longitudinal research shows that the earliest recording of how debt was dealt with goes back to 3000BC during the ancient civilization of Sumer who populated an area that is now modern-day South East Iraq. The book of Chronicles narrated how a debtor who was unable to pay a debt along with their family and servants became debt slaves. They were forced to work for the creditor until such time that their physical labour had repaid the debt. In some cases, it took years to repay the debt, which could even be passed on to the following generation of the debtor's family. Debt slaves became common throughout many ancient civilizations. However, some of the more liberal early societies introduced forms of debt forgiveness or allowed debts to be discharged after a specific period of time. However, Abrahamic religions, discouraged lending and creditors were prohibited from seeking to collect debts.

Before the medieval times, and post Adam Smith, John Maynard Keynes, Milton Friedman etc, businesses and national economies needed finance for expansion, growth, development, or business rescue. The Marshal Plan was an example of continental initiative for European bail out. In the modern times, statistics show that as at 2017, about 2.3 million Nigerians owe banks ₦15.9 trillions. The Asset Management Corporation of Nigeria (AMCON) has expressed that only three hundred and fifty (350) debtors in Nigeria owe it the humongous amount of N3.6 trillion (three trillion, six billion naira). With low productivity, large scale corruption, low savings, and high consumption patterns, Nigerian institutions have had to borrow from local and external sources to bridge gaps in funding, control the national economy and secure maximum welfare, freedom and happiness of citizens on the basis of social justice, equality of status and opportunity.

The Marshall Plan assisted the development of Europe, and regional initiatives like the ADB, NDIC, AMCON have emerged in the loan recovery space. The celebrated case of Salomon v Salomon & Brothers od 1894 came to the fore. Mr. Salomon had transferred his business of boot making, initially run as a sole proprietorship, to a company (Salomon Ltd.), incorporated with members comprising himself and his family. The price for such transfer was paid to Salomon by way of shares, and debentures having a floating charge (security against debt) on the assets of the company. Later, when the company's business went into liquidation, Salomon's right of recovery (secured through floating charge) against the debentures superceded the claims of unsecured creditors, who would, thus, have recovered nothing from the liquidation proceeds.

To avoid an alleged unjust exclusion, the liquidator, on behalf of the unsecured creditors, alleged that the company was a sham, being essentially an agent of Salomon. Since Salomon was the principal, he was personally liable for its debt. In other words, the liquidator sought to overlook the separate personality of Salomon Ltd., distinct from its member Mr. Salomon so as to make Salomon personally liable for the company's debt as if he continued to conduct the business as a sole trader.

For corporations, there are various reasons for debt defaults e.g. like mismanagement, micro-economic headwinds, environmental and political risks, many debtors default in making payments at the agreed time frame or/and debtor(s) blatant refusal to pay preferring to dishonor agreements.

In Nigeria, particularly, the Nigerian state suffers from Quotidian reality "group grievance," "economic decline," "human capital flight," "demographic pressure," "weak and corrupt public service," "deterioration in the rule of law," deterioration in human rights," and "ineffective security apparatus." It may be no exaggeration to add even that "state legitimacy is in doubt." A descent to self-help in debt recovery can translate to a recipe for chaos, which must be prevented by a process of Law.

There are so many reasons why some debtors do not pay their debts as at when due. Some of the reasons include divergence between theory and praxis.

7. The debtor's mismanagement of the loan sum
8. The diversion of the loan sum into unprofitable ventures, even for marrying more wives and for political participation.
9. The debtor may suffer actual inability to pay due to failure of the venture or project for which he borrowed the money. In the Mikibanga's case,[263]

---

[263] Mikibanga & Sons (Nig) & anor. V. African Continental Bank PLC.

the plaintiff debtor obtained an agricultural loan from the defendant creditor bank and mortgaged his house to the bank as security for the loan. He used the loan sum to enhance his poultry farm which indeed was the agreed purpose of the loan. Later, however a mishap set in through no fault of his and he suffered severe loss of the fowls. His poultry business nose dived sharply and as a result, he found himself unable to pay the loan sum.

10. Loans obtained for the purpose of executing government contracts. When this happens, most contractors and business men rely on government patronage and they frequently borrow from banks, institutions and individuals to execute the government contracts. Very often the contractor/debtor may have performed the contract for which he had borrowed money, Government fail to pay him for the contract, eventually he too will become unable to repay the loan sum to the creditor. An illustrative case of the role of government in non-payment by debtors is Nyoyoko v Akwa Ibom State Government & 2ors.[264] The plaintiff had borrowed money from a bank for the purpose of purchasing some typewriters for supply to the then Akwa Ibom State House of Assembly in 1992. After he had supplied the items but before he could be paid, the military took over government and dissolved all civil democratic structures including the State House of Assembly. Even though all the supply / contractual documents were available to the new military government it still did not pay the plaintiff until the plaintiff went to court which ordered payment.

11. Negligence on the part of the debtor or deliberate refusal to pay.

12. Debt.loans as low hanging fruits

2. DEFINITION OF TERMS:

i. Debt:

Debt in the context of this article is a fixed or certain obligation to pay money or some valuable thing or things; either in the present or in the future. In *Eco Bank Plc V Hon Lukpata John Udo*[265] a "debt" was defined as a specific sum of money due by agreement or otherwise." "The action of debt lies where a party claims the recovery of a debt; that is, a liquidated or certain sum of money due him.[266] The action is based upon contract, but the contract may be implied, in fact or in law, as well as expressed and it may be either a simple contract or a specialty. The most common instances of its use are for debts: (a) upon unilateral contracts expressed or implied in fact (b) upon quasi-contractual obligations having the force and effect of simple contracts (c) upon bonds and

---

[264] (2020) LPELR-49691 (CA)
[265] *2012 LPELR-13926 CA*
[266] See Black's Law Dictionary, 8th edition p.432 where the learned authors referred to Benjamin J. Shipman Handbook of common-Law Pleading edited by Henry Winthrop Ballantine, 3rd edition 1923 paragraph 52 page 132 where the learned author wrote that:

covenants under seal (d) upon judgment, or obligations of record (e) upon obligations imposed by statute."[267]

In summary, a debt exists where a certain amount of money is owed from one person (the creditor) to another (the debtor) due to certain agreements. Contracts are entered and executed between parties for various reasons and when there is a breach or failure of party to perform his part of the contract, and a debt arises, the aggrieved party or in this case, the creditor may commence a process to recover the said debt.

The meaning of debt was further defined in the case of *Nigerian Postal Services V Insight Engineering Company Ltd.*[268] *Viz;*

"What then is a debt? I think a useful guide may be found in Jowitt's Dictionary of English Law where the following definition and explanation as to the nature of the "debt" were given. A debt is "... a sum of money due from one person to another. An action of debt lay where a person claimed the recovery of a liquidated or certain sum of money affirmed to be due to him; it was generally founded on some contract alleged to have taken place between the parties, or on some matter of fact from which the law would imply a contract between them. There is aspecies mentioned in the books, called debt in the detinet, which lay for the specific recovery of goods, under a contract to deliver them.... A debt exists when a certain sum of money is owing from one person (the debtor) to another (the creditor). Hence 'debt' is properly opposed to unliquidated damages...; to liability, when used in the sense of an inchoate or contingent debt; and to certain obligations not enforceable by ordinary process ... 'Debt' denotes not only the obligation of the debtor to pay, but also the right of the creditor to receive and enforce payment. Debts are of various kinds, according to their origin ... Debts may be created under the provisions of various statutes.."[269]

ii. A Debtor:

A debtor is **a company or an individual who owes money**. If the debt is in the form of a loan from a financial institution, the debtor is referred to as a borrower, and if the debt is in the form of securities such as bonds the debtor is referred to as an issuer. A person who is in debt or under financial obligation to another is also referred to as a Debtor.

iii. A Creditor:

A creditor or lender is a party that has a claim to the services of a second party. It is a person or institution to whom money is owed. The first party, in general, has provided some property or service to the second party under the assumption that the second party will return an equivalent property and service. A creditor is

---

[267] *Per* **TUR, JCA** *(Pp. 13-14, paras. B-A)*
[268] *2006 LPELR - 8240 (CA)*
[269] *Per* **IKONGBEH, JCA** *(Pp. 22-23, paras. C-D)*

also an entity (person or institution) that extends credit by giving another entity permission to borrow money intended to be repaid in the future. A business that provides supplies or services to a company or individual and does not demand payment immediately is also considered a creditor, based on the fact that the client owes the business money for services already rendered.

v. Debt Recovery:

Debt Recovery is the process of
making people or companies pay the money which they owe to
other people or companies when they have not paid back the debt at
the time that was agreed.

It is also the process of recovering a debt from a debtor(s). This arises when the due date for payment of the debt has elapsed but the debtor has refused to make such payment even when demands for such payment of the loan had been made.

In Nigeria, the limitation period for debt recovery that arises from a simple contract is six (6) years excluding the year the contract was entered into and executed. The court has the power to hear and determine an action for debt recovery and enforce payment on the debtor. The law has provided for a lawful process and procedure for debt recovery. It must be pointed out that owing debt is a civil wrong, and not a criminal wrong. Thus, the Police and other security agencies have no power under the law to arrest, prosecute or to take any action against a person for failure to pay debts.

In the case of McLaren & Ors v Jennings[270], the Appeal Court ruled that debt collection is not part of the duties to the police.[271] The defendants supplied the vehicle used by the police to go to Kano to demand and recover a debt and not for the purpose of investigating an offence. The arrest, in the circumstance, was wrongful. Justice Ayo Salami[272] said in the lead judgment, thus, "In short, the appellants and the policemen they took to Kano were there to collect debt which is not one of the several duties assigned to the police under the provisions of the Police Act to which the court was directed and the court has not been able to find another provision of the Act empowering or constituting the Nigerian Police Force to be one of a debt or rent collector."

The Apex court ruled that issues involving breach of contract are not part of the primary duties of the police, while wondering how the police could "easily metamorphose" a civil matter to a criminal case.[273] Likewise, the Apex court dismissed the conviction of the appellant, who had breached a contract agreement to deliver calf giraffes to the Rivers State Ministry of Culture and Tourism through one Sokari Davies.

---

[270]

[271] McLaren & Ors V Jennings (2002)

[272]

[273] Kure v C.O.P (2020)

Many cases confirm that a cause of action is deemed to accrue when the debtor refuses to pay after a demand is made.[274]

See also Victor v. UBA Plc[275] and Okonta v. Egbuna[276] were referred to for the position.[277]

Progressively the law has sought to ensure free flow of loans for expansion and to ensure economic stability. However, the law ensures provision of capital is not jeopardized in the recovery of their loans so that they can go round to those who require them for socio-economic purposes.

3. Conclusions and Recommendations

i.   The origin of debts shows a cultural transformation from pure agricultural produce, seedlings, money, batter and journey, to predominately money and machines (leasing). The variants have been increasing since the industrial and digital revolutions.

ii.   The subjects of loans and debts remain the same except that institutions and financial structures that give and regulate debts and recoveries vary from country to country.

iii.   For all these categories of participants in loan recovery process, training is needed even for the judges, receivers, liquidators and the debtors.

---

[274] Union Bank of Nigeria Ltd Vs Oki (1999) 8 NWLR (Pt 614) 255, Amede Vs United Bank for Africa Plc (2003) 8 NWLR (Pt.1090) 623." *Per* **ABIRU, JCA** *(P. 36, paras. D-E).*

[275] (2007) LPELR-90413 (CA) Supra

[276] (2013) LPELR-21253 (CA) Supra

[277] Maersk Nig. Ltd. v. Uma Invest. Co. Ltd. (2013) LPELR-21247 (CA), Onokomma v. Union Bank of Nigeria, Plc (2017) LPELR-42748 (CA); Omosowan v. Chiedozie (1998) 9 NWLR (Pt. 566) 477." *Per* **GARBA, JCA** *(Pp. 17-22, paras. E-A)*

The Scope and Nature of the Powers of the Board of Directors under Receivership in Nigeria*

ABSTRACT

Receivership is an enforcement procedure devised by law to ensure that security used for a facility is realised by the creditors. The global meltdown and recession coupled with general political, economic mismanagement have resulted in sub optimal performance of many companies, corporate collapses and also increased defaults in loan servicing especially foreign exchange denominated loan agreements. The importance of receivership has been emphasized and shown to be the most effective forms of enforcement procedures available to debenture holders. This paper therefore seeks to analyse the laws on the appointment of receivers, their disqualification under Companies and Allied Matters Act CAMA[278] and also the lacunae which have provided avenues for encouraging incompetent receivership practices. An attempt has been made to enlighten receivers, courts and managements of the respectively of the boundaries of actions of directors during receivership, the right to derivative actions, and director's right to enforcement of receivers duties as well as claims for breaches of duties of receivers. It has also been expressed that receiverships have tended to encourage self-perpetuating corporate oligarchies especially through government institutional interventions.

1. INTRODUCTION

Generally, a Receiver is essentially an indifferent person between the parties to a cause, appointed by the court to receive and preserve the property or fund in litigation, and receive its rent, issues, and profits, and apply or dispose of them at the discretion of the court when it does not seem reasonable that either party should hold them[279].

Over the years, the process of receivership has developed based on the rules of equity mainly derived from mortgagee's right to take possession of a mortgaged

---

*Dr. Mrs Kathleen Okafor, (Assoc. Prof.) Dean of Law, Baze University, Abuja.
ke_okafor@yahoo.com.
[278] CAP C20 Laws of the Federation of Nigeria, 2004 (CAMA)
[279] Black Law Dictionary; Birch v Wright (1786) ITR 387.

property. At common law, the mortgagee has the right to take possession of a mortgaged property immediately after the execution of the mortgage as a matter of right even where there is no default on the part of the mortgagor. Equity considers the mortgagee in possession to have a trust responsibilities which requires that the mortgagee in possession must account for the actual profits or income made from the mortgaged property, and also for the profit or income he should have made but for his negligence. Due to strict rules of responsibility, the mortgagee preferred to use receivers to possess the property and avoid liability of a mortgagee in possession.

Historically, receivership is an equitable remedy available to both secured and unsecured creditors[280]. Under the common law, the receiver appointed by the debenture holder out of court is regarded as the agent of the company for the purpose of dealing with the assets in receivership[281]. However, currently, the receiver is an agent of the mortgagor even though the mortgagor may have no voice in his appointment nor the power to direct or control his activities or to terminate his appointment. In law and practice, the receiver owes loyalty to the person who appointed him and for the purpose of ensuring the realisation of the security[282]. Under CAMA, receivership is preserved for secured creditors only[283] and receiver is a person appointed only to realize the loan given by the debenture holder(s), while a receiver and manager may realize the loan and also manage the company's business with the same ultimate aim of realising the credit and restoring the company to operations[284].

Usually, a receiver is an agent appointed based on a clause in a debenture instrument or by the court on the application of the secured creditors. Whether appointed by the court or pursuant to an instrument, a receiver owes fiduciary duties to the company and to the creditors to realize the assets of the company for the principal purpose of repaying the secured creditors. The receiver may also be able to return the company to the management of the company when the company attains good financial standing to enable it continue its business or failing which the receiver may turn the company to the liquidator.

The appointment of the receiver either by the court or out of court does not result in the immediate winding up of the company. The company continues in existence until wound up[285].

Corporate borrowings are mainly documented by debentures which are secured

---

[280] Aina Kunle: Rethinking the Duties of a Receiver and Powers of Directors of Companies in Receivership under Nigerian Law; The Gravitas Review of Business and Property Law, June 2015, Vol. 6, No. 2.

[281] Central Land Electricity Ltd v Banners (1985) 1KBD 160

[282] UBA Trustees Ltd v Nigerob Ceramics Ltd (1987) 3 NWLR (pt 62) 600

[283] Hopkins v Worcester & Birmingham Canal Properties (1868) LR 6 Eq 437 @ 447

[284] S. 40 CAMA (1990) NWLR (Pt. 131) 172.

[285] Okoya v Santili, (1990) NWLR (Pt. 131) 172; Intercontractors (Nig) Ltd v NPF Management Board (1988) LPELR SC 94/1987

by a charge on the company's assets. The debentures usually provide events and consequences of default by the creditor whenever there is default by the company. Where the debenture is secured by a fixed charge, the debenture holder, pursuant to the debenture, appoints a receiver or receiver and manager, and where it is charged by a floating charge, the charge will crystallize and the debenture holder will appoint a receiver or receiver and manager as the case may be. Although he is appointed by the debenture holders for the sole purpose of realizing their investments, the receiver is in fact paid by the company for his services. Accordingly, receivership is an enforcement procedure devised by law to ensure that the security is realized by the debenture holders[286].

The advantages of appointing a receiver usually include the following[287];

a.   the receiver helps to quickly and swiftly protect the business and assets of the company thereby safeguarding the debenture holders security

b.   the receiver helps to quickly assess the viability of the company's business

c.   the receiver provides expert monitoring of the company's management and activities on behalf of the debenture holders.

d.   The receiver assists to sell off the company or its equipment as a going concern and assures his appointers of the best price possible in the market, and

e.   affords a better assurance of the return of investment to the debenture holders.

Appointment of a receiver may be made by the court; where there is a fixed or floating charge[288]. The court does not need to wait for the charge to crystallize and become enforceable if satisfied that the security of the debenture holder is in jeopardy. Such situations include events which have occurred or are about to occur which can render or undermine the interests of the debenture holder necessitating exercising the power to dispose of its assets by the company. However, it is necessary for the mortgagee to show that his security is at risk before the court can grant this order. In *Ceramic Manufacturers Nigeria PLC v Nigeria Industrial Development Bank,* the Court of Appeal listed three events that must be proved before the court may grant the order of appointment of a receiver, viz[289]:

a.   that the principal money or the interest thereon is in arrears,

b.   that the security or the property of the company is in jeopardy,

---

[286] Aina K. Supra.
[287] S. 401 CAMA
[288] S. 180 CAMA
[289] (1999) 11 NWLR 383 @ 396 PT. 627

c.   that the appointment of the receiver was made under a power contained in the mortgage deed between the parties

The court must be satisfied of the following salient factors before exercising its power of appointing a receiver:-

- there is in existence a loan transaction between the parties,
- the loan or interest thereon is in arrears and remains unpaid,
- the loan agreement or the deed of mortgage in respect of the loan empowers the mortgagee to appoint a receiver.

It must be explained herewith that the power of the court to appoint the receiver is different from the debenture holder's power under the deed to appoint a Receiver out of court. Thus, section 389(1) CAMA has clarified the issue and requires that the principal sum borrowed or interest must be in arrears or that the security is in jeopardy. Since the provision did not mention the power to appoint a receiver under the debenture deed, it follows that, the court should focus on the enabling powers under the statutory provision. The objectives of intervention by the courts is to protect creditors' funds secured under the debenture during managerial deadlocks, general economic crises etc. and the concomitant negative consequences to the company[290].

In the case of *Fasakin v Fasakin*[291] the Court of Appeal listed the following circumstances when the court may appoint a receiver as follows:

a.   where a company about to be wound up is wholly insolvent and other creditors are threatening action against the company for recovery of their debt; or

b.   where a company was insolvent and its books closed[292], or

c.   where judgment had been secured against a company and execution was likely to issue[293], or

d.   where a company is proposing to distribute among its shareholders a reserve fund which constitutes practically its only asset thereby putting the debenture holders interest at risk, or

e.   where the company's auditors declared in a general meeting and without being challenged by the directors that after providing for liabilities, the company's assets would only cover principal loans secured and that the

---

[290] New York Taxicab Co v New York Taxi Cab Co Ltd (1913) 1 Ch. 1
[291] (1994) 4 NWLR (PT 304) @ 597 SC
[292] Mc Mahan v North Kent Iron works Co. (1801) 3 Ch. 149
[293] Edwards v Standard Rolling Stock Syndicate (1893) San Francisco Call, Vol. 74, Number 97, 5th September 1983, P. 8. 1Ch. 149

company's credit and funds were exhausted[294].

2. LEGAL STATUS OF THE RECEIVER

i. Receiver Appointed by the Court

The receiver appointed by the court owes his duty only to the court and must take custody of the assets of the company and protect them for the benefit of the stakeholders like the creditors and the company. In the case of Jamasons Co. Ltd v Uzor[295], the Supreme Court posited the law on the status of a receiver viz; *'It must be stated that a receiver is not an agent of either of the parties once he is appointed by the court. By his appointment, he becomes an impartial officer of the court whose primary duty is to protect an existing right'*.

Section 389 CAMA provides an elaborate definition of the role of a receiver and the court's power to appoint the receiver whose status, duties and powers are as follows:

> A person appointed a receiver of any property of a company shall, subject to the rights of prior encumbrances take possession of and protect the property, receive the rents and profits and discharge all out-goings in respect thereof and realize the security for the benefit of those on whose behalf he is appointed, but unless appointed manager, he shall not have power to carry on any business or undertaking[296].

Once a Receiver is appointed, the creditors or the directors of the company are not to interfere with the company's affairs as the receiver is an officer of the court[297]. Although section 393(1) CAMA states that the receiver's duty includes realization of the security for the benefit of those on whose behalf he is appointed, the receiver must not work with bias or partiality[298]. He must favour the creditors on whose behalf he has been appointed, and also ensure that he is neutral. By his status, the receiver is not an agent of the debenture holders, although legally appointed on their behalf[299]. Furthermore, the receiver has the power to use the name of the company to institute an action as an agent of the company[300]. He also has the right to institute or defend actions in the name of the company based on the general authority to collect and take possession of the assets of the debenture[301]. The appointment of the receiver puts in abeyance the powers of the directors over such assets until the end of the receivership or until

---

[294] Re Branstien and Majorline Ltd (1914) 112 LT 25
[295] Nashtex Intern Ltd v Habib Ltd & Anor (2007) 17 NWLR (Pt. 1063) 308 CA
[296] ES & CS Ltd v NBB Ltd 2005 7NWLR (PT 925) 215
[297] S. 393(1), Wema Bank Plc & Ors. V Onafowokan & Ors. (2005) 6NWLR (pt 921) 410
[298] S. 390(1&2)
[299] S. 390(1&2)
[300] Solar Energy Advanced Power System Ltd v Ogunnaike & Anor (2008) LPELR - 8470.
[301301] Intercontractors Nigeria Limited v N.P.F.M.B (1988) 1 NWLR P 76 280

liquidation of the company[302].

A receiver appointed by the court remains an officer of the court and not the agent of either the chargor or the chargee[303]. As an officer of the court, the receiver is expected to be neutral. The power of the receiver appointed by the court to maintain an action in the name of the company need not be traced to the agency of the receiver to the company, because under the common law he is not an agent of the company but an officer of the court[304].

Consequently, neither the company nor the debenture holder can control the receiver subject to the receiver's right to be indemnified out of the assets of the company for the liabilities he properly incurs. Legally, the power to sue derivatively in the name of the company is based upon powers derived from the court or CAMA[305]. CAMA specifically states that the receiver is a manager of the company with the aim of realizing the security of those on whose behalf he is appointed. Thus, the receiver remains "in a fiduciary relationship to the company" and shall "observe the utmost good faith towards it in any transaction with it or on its behalf"[306]. The law therefore expects a receiver appointed by the court only for the realization of the security for the benefit of the creditors/debenture holders to be neutral based on agency relationships between debenture holders and receivers appointed out of court under debenture agreement.

ii. Receiver Appointed out of Court

The power of the debenture holder or his trustee to appoint a receiver depends on the terms of the debenture or trust deed. The terms of appointment of the receiver are also normally set out in the debenture or trust deed. Usually, the receiver is an agent of the person or persons on whose behalf he is appointed[307]. However, if the receiver is also appointed as manager of the whole or any part of the undertaking of a company, he shall be deemed to stand in a fiduciary relationship to the company and observe the utmost good faith towards it in any transaction with it and on its behalf. The appointment of the receiver naturally crystallizes any floating charge and has the effect of fixing it over the assets of the company[308]. Under Section 390(1), the receiver is considered the agent of the debenture holder, but if also appointed as receiver manager, he will also stand in a fiduciary relationship to the company. Thus, the appointment of the receiver potentially protects creditors whose interests are covered by some

---

[302] Nigerian Bank for Commercial and Industry v Alfijir Mining (Nig) Ltd. (1999) 14 NWLR (PT 638) 179

[303] Intercontractor Nig. Ltd v NPMB (1988) NWLR (PT 76) 280.

[304] Hayward v Ball (1895) 1 QB 276 CA

[305] Moss S.S. Co. Ltd v Whinney (1912) AC 254

[306] S. 279 CAMA

[307] Tannewa (Nig) Ltd v Arzai (2005) 5 NWLR (PT 919) 5593

[308] Mandilas Karaberis Ltd v Anglo-Canadian Cement Co Ltd (1967) 1 ALR Comm 42, Omojasola v Plison FISKO (Nig) Ltd (1990) 5 NWLR (PT 504) 639.

security or charge over or upon the property of a company in the form of debentures[309]. In this way, the receiver's duty is simply to realize the security and recover the loan on behalf of the debenture holders, whilst the managers' duty includes the management of the company[310]. Under common law, the receiver/manager appointed by the debenture holder is regarded as agent of the company for the purposes of dealing with the assets in the receivership.

In the cases of *Intercontractors Nigeria Ltd v N.P.F.B. and Phamadek Ind. Ltd v Trade Bank (Nig) Plc[311]*, it was respectively stated that the receiver/manager is regarded as an agent of the company for the purposes of dealing with the assets in receivership. In Re Adetona[312], the English authorities on this subject were reviewed extensively which confirmed that the legal status of a receiver is one of agency of the company.[313].

3. Challenging the appointment of a Receiver

The first basis towards challenging the appointment of a receiver is under section 197, CAMA which states that the company or the unsecured creditors must conduct a search at the Corporate Affairs Commission to ascertain whether the debenture was properly executed, registered and also within the vires of the directors and the company or whether the directors complied with the articles of Association of the Company in the entire transaction.

The second basis is that statutorily, the following persons may not be appointed Receiver[314]. Thus, a receiver must be a natural person or a firm of solicitors since a law firm is not a body corporate.

  i.   infants,
  ii. a person found by the court to be of unsound mind,
  iii. a body corporate,
  iv. an un-discharged bankrupt,
  v.   a director
  vi. auditor of the company; and
  vii.   any person convicted of any offence involving fraud, dishonesty, official corruption or moral turpitude and who is disqualified under[315] section 254 of CAMA.

The consequences of contravening the statutory provisions of the qualification of receivers are:

---

[309] See Fasakin v Fasakin
[310] S. 387(1)
[311] (1999) 7 NWLR (PT 514) 639.- Pharmatek Ind. Ltd. V Trade Bank, 36 U.S. (11 Pet) 420, (1837).
[312]
[313] M. Wheler & Co. Ltd v Warren. 36 US (11 Pet) 420, 1837
[314] s. 387 (1) (a-f), CAMA
[315] S. 254, CAMA

134

i.   such appointment is void
ii.   anyone disqualified under section 387(1) CAMA who acts as a receiver or manager shall be guilty of an offence and liable to a fine or six months imprisonment.
iii. The level of punishment imposed under the Act is five hundred naira fine for individuals and two thousand naira for a body corporate.
iv.   There is no liability on the person who appoints a disqualified person. Indeed as the law stands, such an appointor may yet appoint another disqualified person with no liability.

4. DUTIES OF THE RECEIVER UPON APPOINTMENT

Nigerian insolvency regime borrows a substantial part of its underlining precepts from British principles. Thus, Section 390 – 391 of 1986 UK Insolvency Act provides guidance as to the duties of the receiver as:

i.   he must immediately take possession and protect the company's property,
ii. receive rents and profits and discharge all out-goings in respect thereof and
iii. realize the security for the benefit of those on whose behalf he is appointed.

There are the following additional duties where a receiver is a receiver/manager. He must:

iv. manage the business of the company for the benefit of his appointor(s).
v.   give notice to the company of his appointment stating the terms of his appointment. The company will within fourteen days submit a statement of its affairs in a prescribed form to the receiver, who is also expected upon receipt of the statement of affairs from the company to, within two months of the receipt, send a copy to the Corporate Affairs Commission.
vi. send copies of a summary of the statement to the trustees and debenture holders.
vii.   ensure that he submits a report of his receipts and general accounts to the trustees and the debenture holders annually.
viii. a receiver out of court has the duty to constantly seek the approval of the court for his receivership duties. In such actions, the receiver may join the company or a representative of the debenture holders and the trustees if any as respondents to such applications.
ix. a receiver appointed out of court though not an officer of court, may "apply to the court for direction in relation to any particular matter arising in relation to the performance of his functions.

5. DERIVATIVE ACTION AFTER APPOINTING A RECEIVER?

During receivership, the company subsists as a legal entity until wound up and dissolved. Thus, the appointment of the directors of the company does not abate and their services to the company continue. Their powers over the company's assets and business are only temporarily suspended[316]. However, the directors may continue to function as directors of the company only over those assets of the company not covered by the debenture.[317]. The receiver has the power under the schedule 11 to the Companies and Allied Matters Act to bring an action or defend same in the name of the company. He remains the only authority to use the name of the company in actions before the court during the receivership. The directors may however bring a derivative action against the receiver for fiduciary breaches.

Under CAMA, Paragraph V, 11th Schedule. The directors may maintain the action in the name of the company where the directors are challenging the appointment of the receiver as void or irregular.

a.   Actions which do not affect the interest of the debenture holders

The directors may maintain an action on behalf of the company outside the scope and interests of the debenture holders. In ***Oluyori Bottling Company Limited v Union Bank of Nigeria Plc,***[318] the 1st respondent granted the appellant some banking facilities. On the failure of the appellant to liquidate the debt, the 1st respondent appointed the 2nd respondent as a receiver over the appellant. The appellant contended that at various meetings by the parties, the 1st and 2nd Respondents had agreed to pay a certain sum as fees and final payment of the debt and that the 1st respondent appointed the 2nd respondent as receiver in spite of the agreement. The directors of the appellant averred that the appointment of the 2nd respondent as receiver was void and that damages for the properties of the appellant removed by the receiver and disposed of should be paid. The receiver contended that the directors had no locus standi to maintain the action in the first place in view of his appointment as the receiver. The Court of Appeal, held that the directors had the power to maintain the action in the name of the company and that, "Even though the legal powers to dispose of the assets of a company by the directors cease when the company is in receivership, the only powers of the company and the authority of the directors which are affected are those which are within the scope of the charge, but in respect of those which are not within the scope of the receivership and also those where the receiver has refused to act, the company and the directors retain their powers[319].

---

[316] Central Land Electricity Ltd v Banners (1985) 1KBD 160

[317] Mass Steamship Co. Ltd v Whinnay (1912) AC 254; Newhart Dews v Co-operative Commercial Bank (1978)2 QB 814

[318] 2005 8 NWLR (Pt. 928) 547.

[319] Intercontractors Nigeria Limited v N.P.F.M.B

The Court made a crucial statement that also "… as a general principle, although the directors cannot deal with the assets in the receivership, they are not functus officio for all purposes. They are still entitled to exercise their normal functions in other cases not included in the charge".

b. To prevent unjustifiable exercise of receiver's powers:-

The receiver has power to realize the assets and repay the debenture holders which may in some cases, entail taking over the management and selling off of the assets of the company to repay the debenture holders[320].

The company itself, through its board of directors, may sue in the name of the company to check any excesses by the receiver. In the case of *United Bank of Nigeria Ltd v Tropic Foods Ltd,* the Court of Appeal[321], considered whether the respondent company could restrain the creditor from commencing winding up proceedings against the company and appointing a receiver/manager and concluded that the company could do such through the directors.

6. The Scope of Board activities during Receivership

Based on the principle that a company subsists unless eventually wound up, receivership does not dislodge the directors, only the powers of the directors' are put in abeyance[322]. In the case of **U.B.A. Trustees Ltd v Nigergrob Ceramic Limited[323],** the plaintiff was granted syndicated credit facilities by four financial institutions and an all assets mortgage debenture trust deed was executed. The 1st defendant, U.B.A. Trustees Ltd, acted on behalf of the financial institutions. When the plaintiff was not keeping to the terms of the repayment obligations, the 1st defendant in keeping with the terms of the agreement appointed the 2nd defendant receiver of the plaintiff's company and its assets. The board of directors of the plaintiff company met and resolved to sue the receiver. Based on the resolution, the company filed an action against the receiver seeking, inter alia, a declaration that the security had not become enforceable at the time the 1st defendant purported to exercise its power of appointing a receiver under the trust deed, as the conditions precedent to the exercise of such powers had not been complied with. Nnaemeka – Agu JCA gave the following clarification of the scope of the boards power, viz-a-viz the receiver:-

> Such a person (that is receiver) ex hypothesis enjoys powers of management. A man cannot serve two masters; and it would be intolerable if the board of directors and the receiver – manager were to vie with each other to manage the company's business, for the company would not know which direction to follow. At one time it was supposed

---

[320] Fasakin v Fasakin, Supra, S. 383
[321] (1992) 3 NWLR (pt 228) 231
[322] Intercontractors Nigeria Ltd v NPF MB (Supra)
[323] (1987) 3 NWLR 9pt 62) 600

on the basis of the decision in *Moss Steamship Co. Ltd v Whinney*[324] that the appointment of a receiver and manager resulted in the suspension or paralysis for all practical purposes of the directors powers. But it is now clear that the receiver and manager does not usurp all the functions of the company's board of directors. The directors have continuing powers and duties.

The legal position on the continuity or dichotomy of the powers of the directors and the receiver manager can therefore, be summarised as follows;

x. on the appointment of a receiver, the receiver takes over all the assets of the company, including the powers to institute actions in the name of the company, subject to the board instituting an action to challenge the appointment of the receiver[325].

xi. The board of directors can hold meetings and authorize the institution of actions in the name of the company[326].

xii.   The management is no longer in the hands of the board since it has been taken over by the receiver but the board of directors can still validly act in a number of matters, outside ordinary management[327]. This will include challenging the appointment of the receiver by the company, in that the receiver is not expected to authorize action against himself[328].

7. DIRECTORS' RIGHT TO ENFORCE THE DUTIES OF THE RECEIVER

Statutorily, the receiver/manager stands in a fiduciary relationship with the company and yet remains an agent of the debenture holders which are seeming potential opposing camps. The company does not lose its legal personality or its title to the goods under the receivership. In dealing with the assets of the company therefore, the receiver stands in trust and fiduciary relationship to the company in respect of the assets being managed and sold by him. The board of directors of the company in receivership also by virtue of the fiduciary relationship must not abdicate from their duties and must ensure that they monitor strictly the activities of the receiver. As such, whenever there is a breach of fiduciary duties by the receiver, the Board has the inherent powers to institute action for redress. In the case of **First Bank of Nigeria Plc. v Jimiko Farms Ltd & Anor**[329], the appellant banker granted a loan to the first respondent and executed a deed of mortgage in respect of its property in favour of the appellant but failed to meet an obligation under the loan agreement. The appellant, in exercising its right under the deed, appointed a receiver to take over

---

[324] (1912) AC 254
[325] Smith v Middleton (1979) 2All ER 842
[326] WINDSOR Refrigerator Co. Ltd v Branch Nominees (1961) ch. 375
[327] UBA Trustees v Nigergrob Ceramics Ltd (1987) 3NWLR (Pt. 62) 600.
[328] Re B. Johnson & Co. (Board of Directors) 1953 2 All ER 7751
[329] (1995) 5 NWLR (pt 503) 69 @ 93

the management of the first respondent's farms to ensure that the loan granted to the first respondent was recovered. The first respondent then sued for a declaration that he was entitled to account and a claim for the value of the assets taken less the deduction of the first respondent's indebtedness to the appellant. The Court of Appeal[330] observed that the claim had nothing to do with the management of the first appellant but that he was only entitled to the balance of the money collected by the receiver after deducting all the outstanding balance due on its loan. Also, in another case of **Tanarewa (Nig) Ltd v Musa Bala Arzai**[331] the receiver sold off property not directly part of the assets in the debenture deed. The Court of Appeal held that the company through its directors could maintain an action to recover the value of the property sold.

As a manager, the receiver undoubtedly has a duty to act at all times in what he believes to be in the best interests of the company as a whole so as to preserve its assets, further its business, and promote the purposes for which it was formed, and in such manner as a faithful, diligent, careful and ordinarily skilful manager would act in the circumstances[332]. The receiver must act in the best interest of the company as a whole also having regard to the interest of the employees, members of the company, and interests of any class of members or creditors. The receiver cannot contract out of his fiduciary duties and will be held personally liable for any breach of his duties.

Following from the above fiduciary duties and other duties of diligence, the receiver may however be indemnified where he honestly entered into a contract within the scope of the performance of his functions, or with the express authority of the debenture holders, subject to the rights of prior encumbrances[333]. To avoid such fidelity breaches, directors have a subsisting duty to closely monitor the receiver and ensure that the receiver does not exceed his contractual and statutory powers.

7. RECOMMENDATIONS:

a.   The law on enforcement of debentures, generally, and receivership, in particular, needs urgent review and improvement to bring this area of the law in conformity with international standards and global best practices. This is crucial to enable Nigeria reap the benefits of international financing models.

b.   The qualification,   duties and powers of receivers must be clearly streamlinedto avoid current anomalies which permit an all-comers involvement as receivers under the present CAMA. The recognition of insolvency

---

[330] Christlieb Plc v Majekodumi (2008) 16 NWLR (pt 1113) 324
[331] (2005) 5 NWLR (pt 919) 593
[332] S. 390(2)
[333] Christlieb v Majekodumi. (Supra)

practitioners under a professional body may assist in raising the standard of practice and also help in the regulation and monitoring of the activities of receivers.

c. There should be a comprehensive law regulating receivership and insolvency in Nigeria. The Securities and Exchange Commission Rules which regulate trustees generally should specifically extend to the activities of receivers.

d. The current position of making the receiver a fiduciary of both the company and the debenture holder or trustee is nebulous. The receiver cannot also be loyal to the company as he will only be responsible to the person who appointed him with the sole objective of realization of the security. The creation of this conflict of interest and duty is unrealistic and illegal under s. 282 of CAMA, and contrary to best practices.

e. current international receivership architecture is fundamentally out of date as the advanced economies have shaped loan recovery models. The current situation is especially harmful to low income companies depriving them of much needed revenue to help them achieve higher growth, reduce poverty and meet Sustainable Development Goals. The Code of Corporate Governance should specify how companies in receivership should operate with the Board rather than merely stating that the receiver and manager hold fiduciary duties to the company.

f. Continuity of the duties of directors during receivership is commendable as the directors are knowledgeable in the affairs of the company and need to continue to apply their expertise to monitor the activities of the receiver to ensure strict compliance with the terms of the debenture deed. As directors, they alone can prevent the receiver from exceeding his powers, during receivership and steer the ship of the fledging company to safety and profitability.

8. Conclusions

i. Since the law merely specifies those disqualified from being receivers, many receivers lack   professional ethics and apply use of police, paramilitary personnel and extra-legal tactics to take over companies and enforce their presence[334]. Law and due process must be adhered to in order to secure interests of small companies like small and medium enterprises whose business suffer more from like infrastructure deficits, predatory lending practices and macro-economic challenges.

---

[334] TSA Industries Nig Ltd v Kema Investments Ltd (2001) FWLR (Pt. 28) 2174, Abba v Ajoge (1996) 4 NWLR (pt 444) 596.
Ejiofor v Chief S. Onwuagba (1997) 11 NWLR (pt 529) 453, Dagazau v Borki International Co. Ltd (1999) 7 NWLR Pt. 610, 293, Oluyori Bottling Ltd v Union Bank (Nig) Ltd (2008) 7 NWLR Pt 510.

ii. The lacunae of putting restriction on the categories of persons who are appointable as receivers or their qualifications has created jobs for unqualified and unemployed receivers. Elsewhere in the UK and the US, only recognized and registered insolvency practitioners may be appointed receivers. Such eligible persons must also be fit and proper members of recognized and registered professional bodies with requisite education and continuous training.

iii. As the law stands in defining persons disqualified from being receivers, anybody may be appointed a receiver in Nigeria so far as he is not otherwise disqualified under Section 387 of CAMA. However, the law disqualifying directors and auditors of the company from being appointed receivers is salutary to avoid conflict of duty and interest.

iv.Receivers appointed out of court should regularly seek court's approval for their actions to ensure that their actions remain unimpeachable.

v.No person can serve two masters at a time. The receiver appointed by the debenture holder or trustees holds full allegiance to the persons who appointed him and as such cannot practically discharge his duties with the same allegiance or fiduciary zest to the company despite the legal imposition of such duties on the receiver.

vi.Increasing corporate debt amplifies economic downturn as bankruptcies and loan defaults exacerbate existing economic strains, falls in stock markets and heighten financial exclusivity.

www.ingramcontent.com/pod-product-compliance
Lightning Source LLC
Chambersburg PA
CBHW061328220326
41599CB00026B/5084